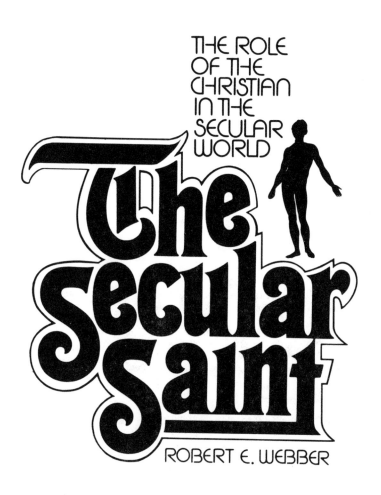

THE ROLE
OF THE
CHRISTIAN
IN THE
SECULAR
WORLD

The Secular Saint

ROBERT E. WEBBER

Academie Books · Grand Rapids, Michigan
Zondervan Publishing House

THE SECULAR SAINT: A CASE FOR EVANGELICAL SOCIAL RESPONSIBILITY
Copyright © 1979 by The Zondervan Corporation

ACADEMIE BOOKS are published by Zondervan Publishing House,
1415 Lake Drive, S.E., Grand Rapids, Michigan 49506

Library of Congress Cataloging in Publication Data

Webber, Robert.
  The secular saint.

  Includes bibliographical references and index.
  1. Sociology, Christian.   2. Christianity and
culture.   I. Title.
BT738.W344   261   79-12181
ISBN 0-310-36641-0

Printed in the United States of America

Scripture references are from *The Revised Standard Version* of the Bible. Copyright © 1946, 1952, 1972 by Division of Christian Education of the National Council of Churches of Christ in the United States of America.

84 85 86 87 88 — 10 9 8 7 6 5

To
Richard Holt, D.D.S.
for showing me the meaning of friendship

Contents

Acknowledgments

The writing of this book was made possible through a grant given by the Alumni Association of Wheaton College. I wish to express a special word of thanks to members of the alumni for underwriting my leave of absence from teaching and for giving me kind words of encouragement and moral support on more than one occasion.

Also, I wish to acknowledge my indebtedness to a number of people who have interacted with me along the way. My student research assistant, Ken Hoglund, proved to be of inestimable value in gathering the sources. My Christ and Culture group leaders and the many students throughout the years who have heard these lectures have given me invaluable feedback. I'm particularly grateful to Carol Griffith for her excellent editing and to Christopher Haas for his painstaking work in preparation of the index. In addition, the specific comments of many people—particularly Richard V. Pierard of Indiana State University, David O. Moberg of Marquette University, and Arthur Holmes of Wheaton College—have helped to strengthen this work.

INTRODUCTION

1

Defining
the Terms

The decade of the sixties produced many changes within
evangelical Christianity. One of these changes was an awakening to our sense of responsibility to be Christians *in the
world.* The movement away from an "other-worldliness" toward a recognition that faith has to do with *this* world came to
a head in the writing of "The Chicago Declaration" in 1973.[1]
The conference that produced this document was both the
expression of and the vehicle for the awakening of a slumber-
ing evangelical social conscience.

Since that time, Evangelicals have written a number of
books about moral, social, and political issues. Why another?

I decided to write this book because I think many
Evangelicals are still confused about how they are to be responsible Christians in the world. This confusion is due, at
least in part, to our failure to have a historical perspective on
the question. For the most part we are calling for social concern without understanding the various ways in which
Christians have functioned in the world in the past.

What I hope to do, therefore, is to set forth the various historic models, show their grounding in Scripture, illustrate them from history, and evaluate their effectiveness in the modern world. In this way I hope both to provide a theology for social concern and to set forth the major models of social awareness that have appeared in the church. The Evangelical who has a good grasp of social theology and the historic models of Christian social action should be in a better position to understand his own responsibility in culture.

In examining this subject we need to begin with some definitions. What do we mean by the words *Christ, culture,* and *models?*

THE MEANING OF "CHRIST"

The word *Christ* calls up many varying images and pictures. Primarily it has reference to a person who lived in the first century in Palestine, was put to death on a cross, and on the third day was raised from the dead. Although this content is basic to all our presentations of Christ and all our discussions about Him, it is only the beginning of what we can say about Him.

While the New Testament community of "Christ followers" accepted these historical facts about Jesus, their understanding of who He was and the meaning of His presence in history went far beyond the mere data that meet the eye. The early Hebraic community of Christians called him the "Messiah." They understood that He was the anointed one, the one predicted in the Old Testament, the fulfillment of the dreams and hopes of Israel, the very presence of God in their midst. The early Greek community knew Him as "Lord." This was a term used in Hellenism to denote a ruler honored as divine, and so it pointed to the recognition that Christ is God.

In addition to these images, the New Testament writers painted portraits of Him that accentuated different truths or various aspects of His personality. For example, Matthew emphasized the royal aspect of Christ; for him, Christ is King. Paul stressed the grace of Christ; John, the love of Christ;

and Peter, the hope we have because of Christ.

This same variety of images of Christ is found in the history of the Christian church. The Catholic church has characterized Jesus as the "man of sorrows"; the Orthodox church emphasizes the resurrected Christ who rules and governs His creation; and Protestants point to Christ as the Savior who forgives sin. Moreover, within these large groupings certain movements have pointed to one particular aspect or another of Christ. The apostolic fathers, for example, stress Christ's role as teacher and the new law-giver; the monastics glory in the humility of Christ and seek to walk in His ways; theologians are concerned with Christ as the content of truth; and the Reformers focus on Him as the only mediator between man and God.

There is also a great deal of variety in the contemporary focus on Christ. The revivalists, for example, magnify the saving power of Christ; the charismatics, His healing power; the existentialists, His judgment on sinners.

Clearly, then, it is difficult to find a term that captures all the images that are descriptive of Christ. The term that comes the closest to it, and the one that we will use in this book, is "the cosmic Christ."[2] *Cosmic* means "relating to the universe," "extremely vast." To specify the term more clearly in its Christian context I offer the following five descriptions. The cosmic Christ is:

1. The Pre-existent Christ. The church has always recognized Christ as the second person of the Trinity, existing with the Father and the Holy Spirit from eternity past. He is, as the Nicene Creed says, "very God of very God." The church has always confessed that His mode of existence always included being "in the form of God" and having "equality with God" (Phil. 2:5-11).

2. Christ the Creator. While heretical Christian groups such as the Gnostics have always attempted to separate Christ from creation, orthodox Christianity has always recognized Christ as Creator. Paul faced the heretical attempt to separate Christ from creation with a resounding affirmation that "in him all things were created, in heaven and on earth, visible and invisible, whether thrones or dominions or principalities or authorities—all things were created through him and for him" (Col. 1:16). For this reason the church has always affirmed the goodness of creation. The world, the cosmos, is to be affirmed. The created order is not profane.

3. Christ as God Incarnate. Paul affirmed that "when the time had fully come, God sent forth his Son" (Gal. 4:4). The church has always taught that Jesus was God in the flesh; in John's words, "the Word became flesh and dwelt among us" (John 1:14). The Council of Chalcedon (A.D. 451) asserted that Christ is "consubstantial with the father in Godhead, and the same consubstantial with us in manhood, like us in all things except sin."

4. Christ the Redeemer. The church has always recognized that God's presence in Christ was for the purpose of redeeming the creation. Paul wrote that "God was in Christ reconciling the world to himself" (2 Cor. 5:19). Both the Nicene Creed and the Chalcedonian definition have at their center the understanding that the Incarnation was "for us and our salvation." The testimony of Scripture and the church is that Christ died and was raised from the dead for our salvation. The writer of Hebrews reminds us that "without the shedding of blood there is no forgiveness of sins" (Heb. 9:22). And Paul reminds us of the effects of Christ's reconciling work on the created order when he tells us that "the creation waits with eager longing for the revealing of the sons of God . . . because the creation itself will be set free from its bondage to decay and obtain the glorious liberty of the children of God" (Rom. 8:19-21).

5. Christ the Lord. Paul declares that because of who Christ is and because of what He has done, "God has highly exalted him and bestowed on him the name which is above every name, that at the name of Jesus every knee should bow, in heaven and on earth and under the earth, and every tongue confess that Jesus Christ is Lord, to the glory of God the Father" (Phil. 2:9-11). When we speak of "the lordship of

Christ," we are referring to His right of reign over the created order, His present reign in the church, and His future rule over all things.

In summary, then, the "Christ" of whom we are speaking in this book is the Christ of orthodox Christianity. He is the "cosmic" Christ, the one related to "all things" by virtue both of creation and of redemption. As we discuss the question of Christ and culture, we will deal with the implications of this understanding of Christ.

THE MEANING OF "CULTURE"

Just as the word *Christ* calls up many images in the mind, so does the word *culture*.[3] Often we think of "culture" in a rather narrow sense, as when we speak of "having culture" or "being a cultured person." Usually "having culture" connotes such things as being pleasant and courteous, having good manners, and generally being characterized by personal niceties. On the other hand, a "cultured person" is thought to be one who has good taste in music, art, and literature, is widely read in current affairs, and upholds standards of moral uprightness.

This approach to culture is sometimes confused with religion. Cultural norms are viewed as the outward expression of religious convictions; therefore Christians are not to have bad habits, and they are to conform to cultural standards in dress, speech, and social customs. Although it may indeed be highly desirable for Christians to be nice, cultured, well mannered, intelligent, and socially aware people, this conception does not get at the heart of the problem of the Christian and culture.

The word *culture* comes from the Latin *colore*, which means "to till" or "to cultivate." It can refer to tilling not only the soil but also the mind, the heart, or the emotions. In the broadest sense, *culture* may be defined as "the total pattern of human behavior and its products embodied in thought, speech, action, and artifacts and dependent upon man's capacity for learning and transmitting knowledge to succeeding generations through the use of tools, language and systems of abstract thought." In this sense it would not be improper to say that culture is the result of "tilling" God's creation.

To be more specific about the way we are using the word *culture* in this book, I offer the following three descriptions:

1. Culture is an activity of man. If man had not been created, there would be no culture. Culture is something that man makes.

In this sense *culture* is a matter of forming nature to man's purposes. It has to do with human achievement through the activity of man's mind and hand. It results in man's organizing himself into social units characterized by communication, transportation, law and order, entertainment, and artistic expression. But culture is not only the noble side of man; it is also the dark side. Violence, greed, corruption, war, murder—the whole unpleasant side of life—are also activities of man that find expression in his culture.

2. Culture is an activity related to the created order. Although culture arises, as we have said, out of the activity of man, there could not be a culture without nature. Man must have something to "till" or form in order to develop culture.

A common mistake is to assume that the created world is given order by man. An order was built into creation by God Himself. The cultural activity of man takes shape within what is already there. That is, all culture is dependent on a prior condition upon which man's activity is exercised.

For example, take language, man's primary means of communication. Languages are numerous, and each living language develops and changes. But language itself, the ability to speak, is not something that man developed or invented. Rather, language is a gift, a part of God's creative act. God made man in such a way that language is intrinsic to what he is. The same can be said for social organization: the fact that man organizes himself into social units arises, not from man's inventiveness, but from the fact that God made him a social being. The same is true in all other areas of man's life, whether economic, aesthetic, juridical, ethical, or religious: they all arise out of, and in respect to, God's act of creation. Thus culture, while it is an activity of man, is expressed only in the context of the created order and is ultimately dependent upon God, who creates.

3. There can be no such thing as a neutral cultural activity. To say this is to recognize the biblical principle that the issues of life proceed from the heart (Prov. 4:23). Man is a spiritual being, and so his activity in the world cannot be amoral. His cultural activities will reflect his values. And values arise from basic religious convictions about life. For example, if what a person values most is the accumulation of wealth, no matter what it costs him, he is unlikely to value honesty, fairness, justice, and concern for fellow man as highly as he should.

In summary, we may conclude that culture results from the activity of man in God's created world. Man unfolds creation and creates a culture that is a reflection of his heart commitment. *Thus the activity of the Christian in culture should be to unfold God's creation according to the purposes of God, so that every area of culture reflects Christian values.*

THE MEANING OF "MODELS"

The word *model* comes from the Latin *modus*, meaning "measure." For our purposes in this book, models are examples of ways by which Christians have lived in the world and against which we can measure *our* pattern of being Christians in the world.[4]

The history of the Christian church reveals many such models, all rooted in a particular conviction about "Christ" and a specific attitude toward "culture." Some of them are well-worked-out models, based on a strong understanding of biblical theology. Others are very weak, based on little or no understanding of biblical theology. Some are mistaken but zealous attempts to follow Christ. Others, because they are derived from a misunderstanding of the biblical Christ or a failure to appreciate Creation and thus man's cultural responsibility, come dangerously close to containing anti-Christian elements.

It is difficult to argue that there is *one* model that puts together all the factors we need to consider in relating to culture. Perhaps this difficulty is due to our fallenness: we cannot do anything perfectly. Yet, because God calls us to perfection, it is our responsibility to consider how we can more fully reflect Christ in our cultural activity.

Here we will examine three types of models:

1. Separational models. These include all attempts to withdraw from the world, either by refusing to participate in the structures of society or by actively creating a counter culture.

2. Identificational models. These advocate participation in the structures of life either by compromising with culture or by recognizing the tension with culture.

3. Transformational models. According to these, the structures of life can be changed either now, through the application of the gospel, or in the future, as the ultimate goal of history.

Questions for Discussion

1. Scan this chapter and write down all those words and terms that are unfamiliar to you. Define them in your own words. What do these ideas have to do with the Christian in culture?
2. What does the notion of the "cosmic" Christ have to do with our relationship to culture?
3. What are some of the things you can do now in culture to unfold God's creation according to his purposes?

Further Reading

Ashaim, Ivar, ed. *Christ and Humanity.* Philadelphia: Fortress, 1970.

Barbour, Ian G. *Myths, Models, and Paradigms: A Comparative Study in Science and Religion.* New York: Harper, 1974.

Buttrick, George. *Christ and History.* New York: Abingdon, 1963.

Eliot, Thomas Stearns. *Notes Toward the Definition of Culture.* New York: Harcourt, Brace, 1949.

Honigmann, John Joseph. *Understanding Culture.* New York: Harper, 1963.

Knoeber, Alfred Louis. *The Nature of Culture.* Chicago: University of Chicago Press, 1952.

Laymon, Charles M. *Christ in the New Testament.* New York: Abingdon, 1958.

Smith, Robert, ed. *Christ and the Modern Mind.* Downers Grove: InterVarsity, 1972.

White, Leslie A. *The Concept of Culture.* Minneapolis: Burgess, 1973.

2

Defining the Problems

A Problem

In 1973 some fifty evangelical Christians gathered at a YMCA building in downtown Chicago to talk about the role of the Christian in society. We divided into groups to talk about such topics as Christians and war, Christians and government, and Christians and race, and I found myself with five others in the section discussing Christians and economic responsibility.

The leader of our group set forth the thesis that every Christian in America should be urged to live on two thousand dollars a year or less. As we talked about this proposal, a distinct group attitude began to emerge: Unless you are unwilling to scale your style of life down to the minimum, you cannot regard yourself as a serious disciple of Christ. After all, didn't Christ say, "If any man would come after me, let him deny himself and take up his cross and follow me" (Matt. 16:24)?

In the midst of all this proposed self-denial, one member

of the group voiced a concern that no one else seemed to have. "I don't think I belong in this crowd," he said. "I'm a businessman—I own my own business—and there's a certain life style I have to maintain. Most of my business is done out of my home. I pick up my clients in my Mercedes Benz, I entertain them with dinner in my expensive home, and I take them for a ride in my yacht to clinch the deal. Last year I gave $35,000 to the church and related organizations. If I gave up my job and lived simply, as you want me to, the church would lose the benefit of that money. So tell me what I am supposed to do."

This businessman's dilemma may be used as an example to illustrate the problem we all face as Christians as we attempt to define our place in the world.[1] (Most of us, however, don't have his specific problem.)

His problem is not that he has a Mercedes Benz and lives in a luxurious home and makes more than $100,000 a year. His problem, like that of all Christians, is that *he lives in two realms simultaneously*. He lives in the realm of culture: he has a family to support, and he has a business that puts him in the world of finance, with its business deals, competition, and, occasionally, unscrupulous men and women. On the other hand, he lives in the Christian realm also. He wants to be a disciple of Christ, he recognizes the need to function by Christian values, and he relates to other Christians in the community of faith. In short, his problem and the problem of all Christians is to find a way to live in both realms at once. How can one operate from a Christian perspective in a dog-eat-dog world? Must he withdraw? Must he function by two sets of values, one in the church and another in the world? Or can his Christian faith be integrated with his role in the world?

A look at the two realms in which our businessman lives will help us realize the complexity of this problem.

First, what does it mean to be "in Christ"? It means, for one thing, that what the man confesses as a Christian must be related to what he does as a businessman. He needs to consider such far-reaching questions as, "In what way is my business conduct related to my belief in the Trinity?" "How do my actions relate to my conviction that God is the Creator?" "To what extent is my life posited on the Christian belief that God is present within His creation?" "How is my life style related to the implications of the Incarnation, reconciliation, the lordship of Christ, the Second Coming?"

Furthermore, if our businessman is to take his faith seriously, he must make decisions about himself and his way of life in the context of those values that belong to the church and those that the church rejects. At what point does his life style reflect greed, lust for power, materialism, covetousness? How can he traffic in the world without becoming corrupted by the unchristian values that are prevalent in the world of business? Can he deal justly, honestly, and with love and still stay alive in the marketplace? To be in Christ means to take all these questions very seriously.

Second, what does it mean to be "in the world"? Our businessman is a cultural being, and so he must consider his problem in relation to what it means to be a human participant in the world. What do his actions have to do with the moral, social, and political aspects of life? How does his way of life bear on the stewardship of energy? How does his consumption of food relate to the problem of world hunger? Might his affluent life style help to perpetuate the imbalance between the rich and the poor? Does it tend toward the creation of a more just society or does it contribute to the perpetuation of injustice?

In summary, the tension that the Christian experiences in the world is the "pull" that results from living in two realms simultaneously. In Christ we are called to selfless love, to servanthood, but in the world mankind operates largely out of selfish interest motivated not by service but by gain. Reinhold Niebuhr caught this tension well in the title of his book *Moral Man and Immoral Society.* No matter how good a person may attempt to be, he is still caught to one extent or another in the corruption of a system that creates and perpetuates evil. And so the Christian is always trapped in that tension between what he is called to be in Christ and what he can actually become in the world. This is the problem of the Christian in culture, and it is one that has vast ramifications, as we shall see.

SOME TYPICAL RESPONSES TO THE PROBLEM

The average Christian does not realize the complexity of the problem of the Christian in culture. For this reason the typical responses to the problem appear superficial and without substance. In general these responses fall into three types: *indifferent, reactionary,* and *pious.*

Those who assume an attitude of indifference would tell the businessman not to worry about the problem. They reflect a kind of stoicism that steels itself against the obvious conflict. They tend to operate with an almost fatalistic approach to life. The conflicts of life are to be simply accepted; we are not to spend much time thinking them through, and we certainly cannot change them. What is called for, then, is a series of compromises and adjustments that maintain the status quo.

The reactionary always takes a "stand," and he takes it in a firm, inflexible way. Broadly speaking, the two reactionary stances that the businessman could take would be (1) turn his back on his work or (2) dogmatically assert that his business is "God's will" and therefore is not to be criticized or changed. In either case the problem would be avoided rather than solved.

The pious response shifts the focus away from the real issue by calling attention to a set of catch-all pieties. The businessman may be admonished to give more to the work of the church and to be sure he doesn't neglect daily devotions, attendance at church, and witnessing in his business.

These responses are prevalent among Christians. I should like to criticize them on two levels.

First, *they are simplistic; they reduce the problem to less than it really is.* Most American Evangelicals, and especially those of us from the white Anglo-Saxon community, are somewhat isolated from the harsh realities of life. Our experience has taught us very little about poverty, hunger, injustice, inequality, disease. We have plenty of food and clothing, and we live in more-than-adequate housing. Most of us have a good-enough education so that unemployment is not a problem, and discrimination against us is rare. It is easy enough for us to assert that we are "in the world but not of the world," to sing that "this world is not my home, I'm just apassing through," to urge one another to "set your affections on things above, not on things on the earth"; but seldom do these formulas reflect a deep personal experience with the problems they are intended to solve.

Yet these easily uttered formulas do point to some truths about the Christian in culture. They do, at least, recognize that Christians are to be different. They reflect to some extent Peter's reminder that we are "a chosen race, a royal priesthood, a holy nation, God's own people" (1 Peter 2:9). Also, there is a sense in which these superficial answers recognize that there is a real struggle in this world with evil. We contend, as Paul reminds us, not against "flesh and blood, but against the principalities, against the powers, against the world rulers of this present darkness, against the spiritual hosts of wickedness in the heavenly places" (Eph. 6:12). Nevertheless, these positive aspects do not counterbalance the weakness of the reduced and oversimplified approach that these typical answers advocate.

In the second place, these typical responses to the problem of the Christian in culture *tend to dichotomize the Christian life. Dichotomize* means "to divide into two parts." The simplistic answers tend to set up a false division between the "secular" and the "sacred." If a Christian does not integrate, or bring together into one, these two dimensions of existence, he or she may live two lives, with neither affecting the other. This situation has tragic results. It pushes the Christian into a kind of super-religiosity. And it encourages him to define his responsibility toward the culture in purely moralistic terms.

The super-religious Christian thinks that it is "sacred" to read the Bible, meditate, pray, witness, and attend church, and that other aspects of life belong to the "secular"—and therefore threatening, if not wicked—realm. Consequently the super-religious deal with life by retreating into a religious shell. They devote most of their time to the activities they know are religious and withdraw from the activities of "the world." Literature, the arts, sociology, philosophy, and other disciplines they disdain as a waste of time in the devil's playground. They lose touch with true humanity, with the problems and needs of an anguished world.

A second result of this dichotomizing tendency is that the Christian tends to see his responsibility toward culture in purely moralistic terms. He essentially says, "Let the world go to hell. Let our energy run out, our air and water be corrupted. Let injustice and hunger prevail. The only thing I am responsible for is my own personal morality." The important issues of life are reduced to such matters as drinking, smoking, dancing, and playing cards—activities from which he carefully abstains. Hunger, poverty, militarism, depersonalization, and a host of other crucial issues are viewed as unrelated to the Christian. The world can go its way as long as the Christian takes care of his personal life.

It is obvious that a person who operates from such a simplistic and dichotomous view of life can offer little to help our businessman. Any advice given will be superficial at best, for it will separate the businessman's life in Christ from his life in the world.

Assessing the Complexity of the Issue

The problem of the Christian in culture is unlikely to be "solved" in the final sense. It is a part of life and as such participates in the incompleteness of life. But we can at least derive some guidelines for response. I wish to suggest three.

First, *life in Christ and in the world is all of one piece.* This guideline is directed against the tendency to set up a false dichotomy between the secular and the sacred. The biblical and theological ground for this argument is found in the church's belief in Creation, the Incarnation, and redemption. If God is the Creator and, even more, if God became man in the Incarnation, then this affirms, or testifies to the validity of, the created order and life itself. Furthermore, because the redemption of Christ is "cosmic," the created order—as well as man—has been, is being, and will be redeemed.

The inescapable conclusion is that all of life is ultimately religious and belongs to God. Religious activity then cannot be limited to pious acts; it must be involved in the whole of life. The businessman dare not assert that his business activity belongs only to the secular aspect of his life. There cannot be any such division. For the Christian all things are sacred.

The second guideline is that *there are two conflicting influences in the world,* two powers at work in our lives. These powers are rooted in the kingdom of evil and the kingdom of Christ. The kingdom of evil operates by greed, covetousness, malice, revenge, and a host of other undesirable impulses. The kingdom of Christ operates according to love, compassion, kindness, lowliness, meekness, forgiveness, forbearance, peace, and other qualities of the Spirit. Life unfolds in the midst of the tension between the pull of the kingdom of evil and the pull of the kingdom of Christ.

A third guideline is that *the Christian must balance three necessary responses to the world he lives in.* These responses are expressed in the three main models for the Christian's life in the world that have appeared in history.

In the first place, he must *identify* with the problem. He is a part of the very thing that he claims to be against. For instance, he participates in materialism, in waste, and in the perpetuation of a system that creates inequality, injustice, and discrimination.

In the second place, however, he must be against the very thing in which he participates. If he is to identify with the kingdom of Christ, he must *separate* himself from an allegiance to the very thing he is identified with. How? Should he withdraw from his work? Or is it enough to be separated from the materialism and greed and other undesirable motives that rule his vocation? Would it be sufficient for him to speak out against the system and seek ways within it to function by Christian values?

In the third place, the Christian must try to find ways to *transform* the structures of life so as to make them more humane, more reflective of Christian values. But how is he to do this? Is he to change existing structures? Or should he create new ones?

In summary, our businessman is caught in a real dilemma. At the workshop in 1973, no one had a really satisfactory answer for him. Most of the committee members told him to sell his business; others thought it was all right for him to stay in business as long as he took care to function Christianly (but no one knew exactly what that meant in that context); still others advocated changing the structures or creating new ones. No one was completely right or completely wrong. Each person was giving one part of a complex three-part answer. A better answer lies in delicately balancing the three responses, not in placing one over against the other.

CONCLUSION

In this chapter I have attempted to introduce the problem of the Christian in culture. It appears to be that of living "in Christ" and "in the world" simultaneously. How do we do it? This question has been answered in three ways: (1) separate from the world; (2) identify with the world; and (3) transform the world.[2]

In the succeeding chapters I will develop the problem and the suggested answers and finally draw some conclusions. In the biblical section I will explore the first of these questions: What does it mean to be "in Christ" and "in the world"? In the historical section I will investigate the three major responses the church has given to the question. And finally, I will attempt to provide a case for evangelical social responsibility.

Questions for Discussion

1. Scan this chapter and write down all those words and terms that are unfamiliar to you. Define them in your own words. What do these ideas have to do with the Christian in culture?
2. We have defined the problem of the Christian in culture as that of "living in two worlds simultaneously." Write down examples from your own experience of this tension as they come to your mind.
3. It has been asserted that "all of life is religious and belongs to God." Give examples of the way you express your faith in areas of life other than church. What, for example, is the Christian approach to your vocation?
4. What would you have said to the businessman?

Further Reading

Cailliet, Emile. *The Christian Approach to Culture*. Nashville: Abingdon-Cokesbury, 1953.

Calhoun, Wallace. *The Cultural Concept of Christianity*. Grand Rapids: Eerdmans, 1950.

Dawson, Henry Christopher. *The Historic Reality of Christian Culture*. New York: Harper, 1960.

Niebuhr, Richard H. *Christ and Culture*. New York: Harper, 1956.

BIBLICAL
BACKGROUND

3

Man as a Cultural Agent

Does the Christian have a responsibility to his culture? Those Christians who tend to see Christianity in purely personal and moralistic terms would say he does not. I believe, however, that he does, and that this responsibility is set forth in the account of man's creation and early history in Genesis 1–11.

In these chapters we find five points that bear on man's cultural responsibility. They are: man's cultural responsibility in the garden, the effect of the Fall on man's cultural activity, the beginnings of civilization and culture, the corruption of man and the destruction of his culture, and the renewal of man's cultural responsibility.

The content of Genesis 1–11 provides, among other things, an interesting and provocative picture of man's place in the world. Commentators, whether they regard these stories as literal truth or as myths pointing to truthful insights about man in the human situation, generally agree that these chapters provide the basis for our understanding of man in culture. Therefore we need not argue here about the validity of these

chapters, nor do we need to enter into the debate about the
origins of the text. Rather, we will accept the text at face value
and examine it to see what it tells us about man's place in the
world.

MAN'S CULTURAL RESPONSIBILITY IN THE GARDEN: GENESIS 1–2

Man's cultural responsibility in the garden is designated
by three terms: "dominion" (1:26,28), "subdue" (1:28), and
"to till it and to keep it" (2:15). All three are to be understood
in the light of the statement "Let us make man in our image
and likeness" (1:26).[1] The idea that man is made in the image
and likeness of God has been called "the magna charta of
humanity" because it affirms man's place in the world.

To understand *why* this idea affirms man's place in the
world, we need to seek out the meaning of the words used to
express it. What does it mean to say that man is made in the
"image and likeness" of God? *Image* in the Old Testament
refers to some formal representation of a god, such as a statue
or idol (Amos 5:26; 2 Kings 11:18), but it can also mean a
copy or a duplicate (see the New Testament usage in Colossians 1:15; compare Hebrews 1:13). *Likeness* is even more
abstract than *image* and is best captured in the idea of re-
semblance. Theologians have disagreed on the exact meaning
of these two terms. Orthodox and Catholic theologians have
separated the two, saying that image refers to man's possession of reason and free will, and likeness to a supernatural
endowment through the action of the Spirit (later theologians
called this "original righteousness"). Most Protestants follow
Calvin in insisting that there is no difference between the two
terms, that they refer to the same thing. Nevertheless, theologians hold in common with Abraham Heschel, an outstanding
Jewish scholar of this century, the idea that "there is something in the world that the Bible does regard as a symbol of
God. It is not a temple nor a tree, it is not a statue nor a star.
The one symbol of God is *man, every man.*"[2]

Perhaps the context itself is the safest guide to the meaning of *image* and *likeness*. Here the words seem to be defined by the phrases "let them have dominion over" (v. 26) and "be fruitful and increase, fill the earth and subdue it, and have dominion" (v. 28). The idea of image and likeness, at least in part, is that since God is sovereign over His creation, man, made in God's image, is to reflect this sovereignty in his relationship to God's creation. Man is endowed with a delegated sovereignty. He has been given the right to rule over creation, to have dominion over other living creatures.

This idea of image and likeness suggests the dignity of man in creation as well as the authority of man over creation. This dignity and authority are specified in a functional way in 2:15, where man is given the responsibility "to till and keep" the garden, and in 2:19, where man names the animals. Here man's creative and imaginative powers are brought to bear on culture. Like God, he does something new. Like God, who without any form or shape to work from brought form and shape into existence, Adam, with no precedent to work with, is expected to give shape to his existence. He is to care for the garden and give names to the animals. This cultural responsibility requires intelligence and creativity. Man is God's unique creation, as the psalmist wrote: "Yet thou has made him little less than God, and dost crown him with glory and honor. Thou hast given him dominion over the works of thy hands; thou hast put all things under his feet" (Ps. 8:5-6).

Just what does it mean for man to have such a high position of authority in God's creation? Here, to some extent at least, we are left with implications from which we must draw our own inferences. I shall suggest three. The first is that man has a cultural responsibility. He is, without question, a cultural being. He cannot escape his essential "belongingness" to this world. He came from the ground and holds a special responsibility toward it. Second, man's cultural responsibility is rooted in the will of God. Man is divinely commissioned to function in culture. To do God's will requires something more than a narrowly conceived personal morality. It means that God's will, which has to do with all of life, is fleshed out by man in the very structures of existence. Third, man's proper response to God is to do God's will. At its most basic level, biblical religion is a response to God. Man may respond either negatively or positively to God's will, but he must respond. Among certain theologians, especially the Reformed, this description of man's cultural responsibility has been called the "cultural mandate."[3] It asserts that man's duty toward the earth is a religious duty, rooted in the will of God.

Man's responsibility to the earth has become a much discussed matter in recent years. In 1966, Lynn White, Jr., a professor at the University of California in Los Angeles, delivered to the American Association for the Advancement of Science a lecture entitled "The Historical Roots of Our Ecological Crisis." In this lecture he asserted that the lack of reverence for nature by industrialized man and the desecration of nature by technology are consequences of biblical teachings. According to White, Western man has interpreted his role as the conqueror of nature for his own benefit. Science and technology therefore express the authority of man over nature.

Rene Dubos, professor at the Rockefeller University in New York, in his Pulitzer Prize–winning book *So Human an Animal*,[4] agrees that technological societies have exploited the earth but disagrees with Lynn White's charge that Western culture has simply applied the biblical maxim to culture.[5] Dubos insists that the technological rape of the earth represents a misunderstanding of Genesis 1 and 2. The Genesis account, he insists, means that the earth has been given to man for his care and that his proper relation to it is one of harmony, not conquest. The idea of harmony does not deny work, nor does it deny the proper use of industry and technology. It simply insists that man work with the earth, not against it.

Man has a cultural responsibility toward the creation. He is called to unfold its treasures and to build structures that are in harmony with the cycles, the patterns, and the order of God's creative act.

THE EFFECT OF THE FALL ON MAN'S
CULTURAL ACTIVITY: GENESIS 3

The burden of Genesis 3 is to describe man's break from the will of God and the effect that break had on his cultural activity. The break with God's will is described in verses 1-7. Eve is tempted by Satan. At first she defends God's restriction against eating the fruit of the tree of knowledge of good and evil. But then she succumbs to Satan's promise that "your eyes will be opened and you will be like gods," which Robert Davidson describes in the *Cambridge Bible Commentary* as "an appeal to that human arrogance which will accept no limitation, which insists on knowing everything."[6] She deliberately "took some and ate." The man ate, too, and together "they discovered that they were naked"—and their innocence was gone.

The effect of that break on man as a cultural being is described in verses 13-19. It includes first a judgment against Satan, the most curious element being the enmity that is to exist between the serpent and the woman; this suggests, perhaps, the shattering of the harmony and peace enjoyed in the garden, its replacement by the conflict of a continued struggle with evil. Second, the woman is judged. She is to bear children in great pain, a symbol that stands as a perpetual reminder of rebellion against God. And she is to be subject to her husband, a perversion of the partnership she enjoyed in the garden. Third, the man is judged. Work, the very nerve of his existence, assumes the character of a struggle. He has to toil for his living against thorns and thistles instead of finding it in a garden of plenty. Even the ground is accursed, suggesting man's alienation from nature. Man and all of creation stand under the judgment of death. Man sought to be like God; instead he found death.

Finally, in verses 20-24, the story comes to a tragic end. God drives man out of the garden, and the entrance to the garden is guarded lest man attempt to return to eat of the tree of life. But two signs of hope keep the story from ending as a total tragedy. First, the woman is named Eve, which means "the mother of all who live"; this points to life in the midst of all that tragedy. And second, God made tunics to clothe Adam and Eve, which suggests that even though the way to the garden is barred, God is still there to meet man's need.

From an interpretative point of view, we may draw a number of inferences. First, man's assertion of his autonomy against God is a decisive break with God's will. As noted in the previous section, man's cultural activity is grounded in the will of God. To break from God's will, as man did, is to assert autonomy from God's revealed will. In the garden man's cultural activity would have been *dependently creative*. That is, man, depending on the revelation of God, would unfold creation according to God's will, in keeping with the order and structure of the universe, and this unfolding would reflect the harmonious relation between man and God. But man's assertion of autonomy, his break from God, put him in a position where he became *independently creative*. That is, independent of God's will, and even independent of the order and meaning in the structure of the world, man set out alone to unfold culture. Consequently his cultural activity has, in every aspect of his life, reflected his break with God's will. The disharmony in his life is the result of that assertion of independence.

Second, the assertion of man's autonomy against God disturbs the harmony and peace of the garden, introducing new and disruptive forces into man's existence. Here is the root explanation, not only for the break that exists between man and God, but also for man's alienation from himself, from his neighbor, and from nature. Hate, greed, violence, war, immorality, drunkenness, jealousy, rivalry, strife, selfishness, and all the other disorders that plague man's existence are rooted in his break from God. Man's attempts to rule and harness nature without respect to its order, rhythm, and cycles are acts of aggression against the creation, ultimately rooted in his rebellion against God. Further, man now enters into a struggle, a wrestling not "against flesh and blood, but against the principalities, against the powers, against the world rulers of this present darkness, against the spiritual hosts of wickedness in the heavenly places" (Eph. 6:12). And finally, man and all his works are brought under the judgment of death. Death, the disintegration of man's whole existence, the final and ultimate judge of life, now stands over life as its final mockery. Man's break with the will of God is no illusion.

Third, even though man has asserted himself against God, God's disposition toward man is still one of grace. The image of God in man is not totally destroyed—it is only marred, defaced, distorted. Man can still function humanly. He is corrupt and violent, but not so much so that he is incapable of acts of kindness, of love, of caring. Here and there man's actions provide us with a glimpse of his capacity, not only to function humanly, but also to perform constructive and creative acts of goodness that benefit mankind. Man is not an animal; though off course from his original direction, he is still made to function in God's image.

Finally, from a contemporary point of view, the content of Genesis 3 is no isolated piece of history. It has immediate relevance to our situation, standing as an explanation of our current problems in such areas as ecology, racism, feminism, hunger, and war. It is a truth for our times, for it helps us to see ourselves in the perspective both of God and of history. We are what we are because we have broken away from God's will. And the history of culture, as well as the turmoil of our own times, witnesses to our alienation.[7]

THE BEGINNINGS OF CIVILIZATION
AND CULTURE: GENESIS 4

All the material from Genesis 3 through 11 can be seen as the writer's attempt to show, as Gerhard Von Rad suggests, "a chain of actual events, a road which mankind took."[8] Here, in Genesis 4, the narrator as part of the chain chronicles the beginnings of man's spread throughout the earth. His purpose is theological—to show how the breakdown of the harmony that once existed between man and God has led to tragedy in human relationships. Man, who asserted himself against God, now asserts himself against man.

Cain, the object of verses 1-16, commits the first crime against his brother. His attempt to hide it from God is unsuccessful. Because the ground has received Abel's blood, Cain is cursed from the ground. It will no longer yield to him its strength. Furthermore, he is to become a wanderer and a fugitive on earth, a homeless outlaw. Yet, though he is cursed and outlawed, Cain is not separated from the protection of God, who places on him a mark to indicate that he is protected. Cain goes away from the presence of the Lord to dwell in the land of Nod, east of Eden. The Hebrew word *nod* means "wandering" and is found nowhere else in the Old Testament as a place name. It conveys the idea that, as Davidson puts it, "Cain has become a 'homeless wanderer,' out in the far distant, unknown region, east of Eden."[9]

The material in verses 17-24 is the first of a series of "family trees," used to describe both the passing of generations and characteristic features of life. Here in capsule form is a description of the advancement of civilization. The origin of cities, a settled community existence, is traced to Cain. Momentous changes take place in culture—herdsmen, musicians, and smiths begin to appear throughout the land. The last of these changes introduces the sword, something new, and the narrator concisely shows how this new invention entices man to evil (22-24).

Even in this narrative there is hope. Man is not left destitute, without God. Hope is expressed, not through Cain but through Seth, the son who replaces Abel. For at that time men began to call on the name of the Lord (25,26). Chapter 5 then provides the link between Seth and Noah.

From an interpretative point of view, this passage is a rich source of insight into man's cultural beginnings. Perhaps the most instructive thing to notice is the *paradox of man's cultural beginnings*, which reflects the paradox of man's existence, what Augustine referred to as the two cities—the city of God and the city of Man: Cain, who went away from the presence of God; and Seth, who began to call on the name of the Lord. In these two lines of humanity and cultural development are to be found the ever-present tension between those who desire to unfold culture autonomously, without respect to God, and those who wish to unfold culture in keeping with the will of God.

1. The line of Cain. In Cain's line of descent there is a bent toward violence. Cain treated his brother's life with no ultimate regard for life itself. He cared only for himself, and when God called him to answer for it, he refused to admit any responsibility for his brother, asking, "Am I my brother's keeper?" This same kind of refusal to become involved in caring for one's neighbor is reiterated in Lamech: "I have slain a man for wounding me, a young man for striking me." Violence is at the heart of culture not only here in the Genesis narrative but in the whole history of man's existence. The explanation given in Genesis is that violence is rooted in man's break from God and in his subsequent refusal to care for his neighbor.

Cain's line of descent is also characterized by its homelessness, its rootlessness. From our text we gather that this is a result of man's violence and refusal to care for his brother. Cain is a fugitive and a wanderer on the earth. The emphasis here is not that Cain became a nomad but that he was driven away from the ground and from the face of the Lord. The inference is that he was cut off from the source of his life—the ground and God. It was the absence of meaning, the absence of a transcendent reality, that Cain suffered. Driven from the presence of God because of his break with God, he was left to find his own way in life. In this sense, Cain represents the human condition. Without God's presence, man is left on his own, searching and groping to find meaning, purpose, and direction in life. Cain left "the presence of the Lord, and dwelt in the land of Nod, east of Eden." Here, says Jacques Ellul, "he is condemned to a perpetual searching for God's presence, the God with whom he wanted nothing to do and in whom he does not believe, and his very condition keeps him from ever finding him."[10]

It is in this context that Cain "built a city." There is, of course, nothing intrinsically evil about building a city. But this city was built by one who had chosen to move "away from the presence of the Lord." Cain's unfolding of culture was not in the direction of God but away from God. Evil, therefore, is not in the construction of the city but in man, who independently of God constructs his city. Consequently the violence and the rootlessness of man's nature will be reflected in what he builds. The city will become a personification of man's evil; violence, bloodshed, and homelessness will be characteristics of its life.

2. *The line of Seth.* Very little is said about the line of Seth, perhaps because the main purpose in introducing Seth is to draw a line between him and Noah, as the genealogy does in chapter 5. Nevertheless, there are two instructive things about the mention of Seth and the genealogy. The first is that in the days of Seth "men began to call upon the name of the Lord" (4:26). The second is the brief description of Enoch—he "walked with God" (5:24).

Here, then, is the other side of the coin. There are in culture those who, unlike Cain, have not broken with the presence of God. This line, though a minority, constitutes those who remain faithful with God and desirous of living life in response to His will. Little is known of Seth and his line except that they remained sensitive to God's will. Obviously we are to assume that these people were a part of the emerging culture, that they were involved in building cities, farming, tending the cattle, making music, forging instruments, and the like. But, unlike the line of Cain, they sought to unfold their personal and cultural lives in conformity with the will of God.

From a contemporary perspective, the narrative of the two lines of cultural beginnings provides us with a way of looking at our cultural situation. In every society and culture there is a mixture of people: those who wish to unfold their lives and the life of their culture according to the will of God, and those who, having broken with God, desire to become the masters of their own fate.

The two types, however, are not always so distinguishable as it would appear from our narrative. Some who claim to love and serve God support violence; some who have broken with God are humanitarian and deeply concerned about their fellow men. Fallen man is not so depraved that he is incapable of doing good deeds, and redeemed man is not so thoroughly redeemed in his life style that he cannot do evil. The distinction between the line of Cain and the line of Seth is not so clear-cut that we can say, "Here is the one and here is the other." No, the two lines represent paradoxical elements that are found in each one of us and in our culture. To the extent that one loves or cares for his neighbor, one does the will of God. And to the extent that one hates his neighbor and treats him badly, one does not do the will of God. What the text is describing, then, and what we experience in life, is the tension between doing the will of God and not doing the will of God, moving toward God and moving away from God. Both of these tendencies are evident in every culture. But the Christian is especially called to live by the one and not the other. He is to unfold his life and the life of his culture after the pattern of Seth.

THE CORRUPTION OF MAN AND THE DESTRUCTION OF HIS CULTURE: GENESIS 6–8

The extent to which sin permeated the whole of man's existence is the subject of the narrator's concern in Genesis 6–8. Here we see the consequence of building a culture "away from the presence of the Lord."

To begin with, the narrator places the flood story within an ethical context (6:1-8). Man's wickedness "was great in the earth, and . . . every imagination of the thoughts of his heart was only evil continually" (6:5). Here the writer provides us with his own commentary on the human situation, giving us insight into the extraordinary extent to which sin had permeated the structure of man's entire existence. But he places the responsibility on man, who because of his neglect of God's will has brought this bad situation on himself. Nevertheless, in his prologue, which emphasizes judgment, the writer rather subtly points to two other themes, salvation and covenant, that are rooted in God's favor and Noah's obedience. The world, as bad as it may seem, is not without hope.

Clearly, though, the spirit of Cain, and not that of Seth, dominated the world of men, so much so that the world had become corrupted and the end to which this would lead had become inevitable (6:9-13). That the world had already destroyed itself through its own violence and that God's irrevocable judgment was only a carrying through of the inevitable is seen in the meaning of the Hebrew words translated "corrupt" (6:11-12). They come from the same word, the word meaning "destroy" (6:13). The implication is that the world that God will destroy has already destroyed itself through violence. Man has dug his own grave.

In contrast to the world of corrupt men, Noah was one who had "walked with God" (6:9) and was "righteous before [him]" (7:1). Noah was obedient to God: he "did all that God commanded him" (6:22; 7:5). The narrator carefully emphasizes God's care for Noah. The Lord not only instructed him to build the ark but also "shut him in" (7:16)—closed the door for him—and "remembered" him (8:1). Here we gain a second insight into the very heart and character of God. The first was that He was grieved (6:7); He was sorry that He had made man. The second is that His love and care continued—He "remembered." This word, as used in the Bible, means not merely that the past was recalled by God but that it served, to quote Davidson again, as a "spring-board for his present outgoing activity."[11] It means that God is going to do something new (see especially Genesis 2:24 and Luke 1:72 ff.).

The thing that God is going to do is to make a new creation. He is going to start over again with another conquest over the watery powers of chaos (8:1-3). In this sense the Flood makes a major turning point in the history of man and his culture. The implications of this material for our understanding of the Christian in culture are many and varied. I will mention four. First, it implies that sin permeates the whole of man's existence. We sometimes tend to think that sin is nothing more than individual acts against God. But here the text suggests that man's cultural unfolding reveals that the entirety of his social and cultural life is affected by sin. Sin finds institutional expression. It affects our politics, our economic commerce, our aesthetic products, and our relationships to one another, to mention only a few areas. Our participation in life, then, incriminates us as being party to the oppression, injustice, cruelty, and violence of a system not obedient to the will of God.

The fact that he is a seemingly unwilling participant in the human institutions and systems that reflect man's sinfulness in no way relieves man of his responsibility for that sin. This is clearly suggested in the Genesis flood narrative by the writer's insistence that the responsibility for evil rests on man's shoulders. Man is not made evil by his environment. He makes his environment evil because, unlike Noah, he is not sensitive and obedient to the will of God.

The consequence of his sin is that he sets the course of history toward self-destruction. This theme, which recurs many times in the Old Testament, especially with the destruction of the northern and southern tribes of Israel, is cited again by Paul in Romans 1. God's judgment against man is never arbitrary. God simply turns man over to his own inclinations and allows him to destroy himself. Man sets his own course and determines his own end when he deliberately and willfully elects to unfold his life and that of his culture without heed to the will of God.

Nevertheless, God does not turn His back on man. He is there, prepared to begin again, to start a new creation, to give man another opportunity.

This passage is as pertinent today as it was in the writer's time. By our so-called technological expertise we have, it seems, built a world that is now suffering from acute overload and shortage.[12] While some see a way out, others are quite

convinced that a tragic ending is inevitable—that it is only a
matter of time.

THE RENEWAL OF MAN'S CULTURAL
RESPONSIBILITY: GENESIS 9–11

In Genesis 9–11 we move beyond the tragedy and judgment of the Flood to the hope for mankind that is established
through a new beginning. Because the new cannot be a mere
repeat of the old, the emphasis of the narrator in 9:1-17 falls on
the problem of man and the disturbance he brings into the
natural order.

As in the first beginning, man is to "be fruitful and multiply, and fill the earth" (9:1). But the original verdict that
creation is "very good" (1:31) is no longer heard, for the
harmony of creation has been shattered. Consequently, the
animals who once came to man to be named now flee from
him, and man, who was once a vegetarian, now eats the flesh
of animals.

Two restrictions on man's lordship over creation now
appear. First, he is not to eat flesh containing blood (9:4).
Because blood is equated with life, this restriction may im-
press on man the fact that he cannot do whatever he wants
with life. Life belongs to God, not to man. This same theme,
even more strongly put, controls the second restriction: man is
not to take the life of man. The penalty for murder is death
(9:6). Interestingly, the death of the murderer is to be accomplished by man. Although no attempt is made here to describe
any institution by which this is to be done, the passage does
seem to suggest the principle of human government along with
that of the sanctity of human life. Life is worthwhile, and
therefore it is to be protected.

The next new note that enters into man's beginning-
again is that of the covenant. It is a covenant, not merely
between man and God, but with the descendants of Noah and
every living creature (9:9-10), pointing to the whole of man's
existence. It is an everlasting covenant (9:11) established with
endless generations (9:12), reaching therefore through the en-

tire history of man and pointing to the ever-present reality of God's presence in life. And it is confirmed by a sign in the heavens, something that points beyond man's rational power of explanation to some aspect of God's nature or activity, in this case to the *dependability* of God.

The roll call of nations in Genesis 10 looks both backward and forward. In the sense of looking backward, the narrator uses it to show that God has fulfilled His commands to Noah to be fruitful and increase and fill the earth (9:1). In that way it connects all the families of the earth to one man, and thereby helps to explain the forward thrust. For while all men come from Noah, only one line of descent has religious significance, and that is the line leading from Noah to Shem, from Shem to Abraham, and from Abraham to Israel. Politically, Israel may be only one among many, but theologically it is the one on whom the hopes of the world are pinned (as the narrator later develops the thought).

This idea is given further credibility by the story of the Tower of Babel. For here the importance is found, not in answering a mundane question like "Where did all the languages come from?" but in pointing to man's desire to glorify man by making an edifice that would "make a name" for themselves (11:4). The outcome of man's desire to worship and glorify man is division, confusion, and chaos. The whole family of man is searching for security and meaning apart from God, but within that otherwise hopeless situation is the line of Seth (now Shem)—a people of God within culture who give hope to the world.

From an interpretative point of view, three things emerge here. The first is the narrator's subtle attempt to develop the idea that there is a people of God in culture different from the rest of the people in the world. Although this idea is only in germinal form here, the writer's concern to provide a setting for Abraham and the call for a separate people of God is made obvious by what follows in Genesis 12. Secondly, the need for human government as a means of controlling man emerges in respect to murder. The need for government is further implied by the confusion of tongues at Babel. Thirdly, despite the new beginning, man is portrayed as unable to unfold culture after the will of God. His rebellion and his desire to please himself are still an intrinsic part of him in the new beginning.

CONCLUSION

The themes of Genesis 1–11 provide the biblical background from which our considerations of man in culture, as well as God's people in culture, emerge. Here the transcendent God creates man and gives him a cultural responsibility—the care of the earth. But man, rebelling against God and His will, continually seeks to make himself and his own desires central to life. This desire results in confusion, chaos, disorder, and finally judgment. Nevertheless, God is always at work in history, pointing beyond man's disastrous unfolding to new possibilities. This theme, undeveloped in the Genesis 1–11 narrative, will become a major one in the emergence of Israel as the people of God in culture, pointing to the possibilities of life and ultimately to the Messiah, His kingdom, and the new heavens and new earth. Through this interplay of God and man, and man in God's world, we can ultimately gain some insights into our role in the world.

The model of man's role in culture appears in Genesis 1–11. There are certain fundamental precepts that have to do with this role:

1. Man's religious life is not divorced from his cultural responsibility. His response to God, rooted in the will of God, is expressed in the way he unfolds life culturally.

2. Man's break from the will of God is reflected, not only in a broken relationship with God, but also in the perverted relationship that now exists between man and his fellow man and between man and nature, as well as in an inner break that man has made with his original self. Consequently, the variance of man with the whole of his existence finds acute expression in the unfolding of culture.

3. The judgment of God against man's rebellion is present in the very structures of existence. But here, too, in the establishment of a people who do God's will, there is the hope of a new direction in cultural unfolding.

We turn now to an examination of how God's people failed to fulfill their cultural responsibility and to the hope of the kingdom, when man's cultural responsibility will be finally fulfilled.

Questions for Discussion

1. Scan this chapter and write down all those words and terms that are unfamiliar to you. Define them in your own words. What do these ideas have to do with the Christian in culture?
2. It has been suggested that man has been given the right to rule over creation, to have dominion over other living creatures. What does this mean? Can you give some examples of the improper approach to this idea? What do you think is the proper relationship of man to creation?
3. Can you discern the lives of Cain and Seth in the world today? Should you be able to?
4. We have asserted that "sin finds institutional expression." Give some specific examples drawn from your experience, reading, and general knowledge.

Further Reading

Dubos, Rene. *So Human an Animal*. New York: Scribner, 1968.
Elder, Frederick. *Crisis in Eden: A Religious Study of Man and His Environment*. New York: Abingdon, 1970.
Ellul, Jacques. *The Meaning of the City*. Grand Rapids: Eerdmans, 1970.
Heschel, Abraham J. *Between God and Man*. Edited by Fritz A. Rothschild. New York: Harper, 1959.
Von Rad, Gerhard. *Old Testament Theology*. New York: Harper, 1962.

4

The Context of Cultural Activity

We have seen, up to this point, that man as the image-bearer of God is called to act as cultural agent in God's world. In this respect the religious life of man is more than that which cultivated the "soul." It has to do with the whole of life.

But man's religious activity does not take place in a vacuum. It is not as though he has no guidelines, no blueprint, no principles to follow. God has not put man into the world to unfold culture according to man's whim or fancy. No, God Himself has a plan, a purpose for His world, and man's place in the world is to act as a cultural agent within the context of God's purpose.

The key to understanding this purpose of God is in the biblical concept of the kingdom of God. The kingdom is a very complex idea, and we cannot delve into it deeply; to do so would carry us afield from the purpose of this book.[1]

The concept of the kingdom of God involves the total message of the Bible. One cannot understand the central theme of redemption apart from the idea that God has called out a people to live under His rule and that these people are directly related to the hope of the kingdom. The fact that they must live *in the world* and that God has given them specific directions about this life in the world is the crucial point for our discussion. God's people have a cultural calling. They are to show by their activity in the world that they belong to the kingdom of God. Therefore, if we are to understand the role of the Christian in the world, we must understand the kingdom of God.

The kingdom of God is the dominant theme in the preaching of Jesus. It is striking, however, that He never attempted to define what He meant by the kingdom of God. Why? The answer is that the Jews all had an understanding of the kingdom. The hope of the kingdom was part of the warp and woof of their life. They lived in anticipation of its coming.

This hope of the kingdom involved what John Bright has called "the whole notion of the rule of God over his people, and particularly the vindication of that rule and people in glory at the end of history."[2] Central to this hope was the coming of the Messiah. But all of this was only gradually known in the history of God's people in the Old Testament. Therefore, to get a grasp of the whole idea of the kingdom of God as it bears on cultural responsibility, we will have to go back to the beginnings of Israel, back to those people who were chosen by God to be His people. Then we will look at Jesus' own understanding of the kingdom and His place within it. And finally, we will inquire about the relation between the kingdom and the church.

THE KINGDOM OF GOD AND THE OLD TESTAMENT

The term *kingdom of God* does not appear in the Old Testament. How then can we speak of "the kingdom of God *and* the Old Testament"? The justification lies in the fact that the idea is broader than the term. Because the idea of the kingdom involves the whole notion of the rule of God over His people and the anticipation of God's complete rule over His creation in the end time, it is appropriate to apply the term generally to the Old Testament people of God who are brought under His rule. It is here, in the covenant relationship between God and Israel, that the idea of God's rule over a people is given substance. Through the covenant we gain our first insight into those cultural responsibilities that are given to the people of God.

The people of God are called into being as a cultural entity in the exodus event. God's leading the descendants of Abraham out of Egypt, through the Red Sea, and to Mt. Sinai, where He enters into a covenant with them, is the most momentous event of the Old Testament. Three of its many implications are important for our study.

First, through this event a crucial and basic fact about God is made clear: it is now known that God is in control of history and that He is known through historical events. This fact about God sets Him sharply apart from the pagan gods. For the most part, pagan gods were mere personifications of the forces of nature who could be manipulated or controlled through ritual. But the God of Israel controls history and through it calls men into obedience to Himself.

Second, because God chose a people and worked in history on behalf of them, it was recognized that God had a historical people. Says Bright, "The notion of a people of God, called to live under the rule of God, begins just here, and with it the notion of the Kingdom of God."[3]

Third, the covenant made between God and Israel made it very clear that God's people were a people in history with responsibilities toward God and their neighbors. They were a people with cultural responsibilities.

The contractual arrangement between God and Israel makes this clear. "Moses came and told the people all the words of the LORD and all the ordinances; and all the people answered with one voice, and said, 'All the words which the LORD has spoken we will do'" (Exod. 24:3). In the covenant, God agreed to be the God of Israel and Israel agreed to be His people and *to live under His rule*.

This rule of God for His people included keeping the

words and the ordinances. The *words* appeared in two tablets. The first dealt with the Israelites' duties toward God and the second with their duties toward their fellow men. These words became, therefore, the constitutional basis from which the whole religious and moral life of the people of God sprang. The *ordinances*, which were the rules of the covenant code, were part of the specifics that sprang from the more general principles set forth in the words (Ten Commandments).

The point to note for our purpose is how closely tied to cultural responsibility these ordinances are. They specify how God's people are to function in the world:

> "When you buy a Hebrew slave, he shall serve six years, and in the seventh he shall go out free, for nothing" (21:2). . . . "Whoever strikes a man so that he dies shall be put to death" (21:12). . . . "You shall not wrong a stranger or oppress him, for you were strangers in the land of Egypt" (22:21). . . . "You shall not afflict any widow or orphan" (22:22). . . . "If you lend money to any of my people with you who is poor, you shall not be to him as a creditor, and you shall not exact interest from him" (22:25). . . . "You shall not follow a multitude to do evil; nor shall you bear witness in a suit, turning aside after a multitude, so as to pervert justice; nor shall you be partial to a poor man in his suit" (23:2-3).

We may conclude that in the exodus event God showed Himself to be in control of history and created a historical people over whom He intended to rule. One way in which His rule over this life is expressed is in terms of His people's responsibility in culture. At this point *how* they are to be related to culture is not yet clear. What is clear is that their obedience to God is both personal and social.

The history of Israel is an account of Israel's success and failure at being the people of God in culture. It is not within the scope of this book to give a full account of the history of Israel or to explain the problems that are raised as the result of God's cultural directives (annihilation of people, wars, and miracles). We do need to look, however, at the highlights of Israel's cultural involvements and to its failures and successes in upholding the original covenant with God. Specifically, three periods are of interest: the conquest, the Davidic era, and the divided kingdom.

First, in the conquest, God demanded that Israel rid the land of *all* the Canaanites and possess the land wholly for themselves. They were to expect great things of God in the future as long as they were obedient to Him. He would defend them, go before them, and lead them victoriously into the Promised Land. They were a people with a destiny, a future. In this consciousness we may find the seeds of the kingdom hope. If they were obedient to God, He would bring them into the Promised Land and establish them as His people.

The nature of the people of Israel as possessing a culture separate from the culture of the Canaanites was clearly set forth in the conquest. But the Israelites failed to destroy the Canaanites completely and instead intermingled with them. They became conquered by the people they set out to conquer, because they did not completely obey the word of God through Joshua not to mix or intermarry with the Canaanites. In succeeding years a series of judges rose up and led certain tribes to occasional victory over the Canaanites as well as restoring short-term obedience to the covenant. But the Israelites wanted to have a king as the other nations did, and God granted them this desire in Saul, David, and Solomon.

Under David a transformation of culture took place. The people of Israel were no longer a loosely connected group of tribes but were now a kingdom. Religion and culture flourished. The golden age of Israel had arrived. It was as though the promise of the Abrahamic covenant had been fulfilled. More than any previous culture, the culture that they produced reflected an obedience to God's words and ordinances. It was good to be an Israelite under David. The people enjoyed material prosperity and what seemed to be the obvious blessing of God in return for obedience.

But the golden era did not last long. Conditions began to deteriorate under Solomon, and in time the nation split into two parts, the north and the south. Soon an unfortunate identification with false gods, a desire for material luxury, and greed replaced a commitment to the covenant. The covenant was disregarded, the worship of God became sterile, and the

people grew cold and indifferent. God met this indifference
with judgment. First Israel fell, then Judah. The people of
Israel were brought under the rule of one nation after another.
Israel had failed miserably to keep the covenant with God. Its
culture had not been shaped by an obedience to the will of
God.

The point is that what God expected of Israel was an
obedience to His will within culture. God's rule over Israel
was to extend into every aspect of their living.

Israel's disobedience was more than an internal private
and personal disobedience. The prophets point to its *cultural*
shape. An example is found in the admonition of Amos:

> "Thus says the LORD: 'For three transgressions of Israel and for
> four, I will not revoke the punishment; because they sell the
> righteous for silver, and the needy for a pair of shoes—they that
> trample the head of the poor into the dust of the earth, and turn
> aside the way of the afflicted; a man and his father go in to the
> same maiden, so that my holy name is profaned; they lay them-
> selves down beside every altar upon garments taken in pledge;
> and in the house of their God they drink the wine of those who
> have been fined'" (2:6-8).

The concern that is cited again and again is that Israel's
disobedience is a refusal to live under God's rule—a willful
rejection of God's expectations for living in the world (see Isa.
26:9; Jer. 21:12; Mic. 3:1). Israel's disobedience is clearly seen
in its culture.

Having seen that obedience to the will of God is expressed within culture, we return to Israel's history to see how
the kingdom idea took shape. There are six themes related to
the kingdom idea that we need to grasp as background to the
relation between the kingdom and the role of the Christian in
society. They are: the Davidic ideal; the prophetic voice; the
new covenant; the hope of a new Israel; the suffering servant;
and the apocalyptic hope.

The Davidic ideal. The zenith of spiritual and material
prosperity in Israel occurred under David. During his reign
the people of Israel had come the closest to fulfilling their role
in culture as the people of God. The Davidic era therefore

remained strong in the minds of the people and became more than a memory—it became a *hope*. The hope of Israel was that a king would rise in the line of David to establish a kingdom like David's that would last forever (see 2 Sam. 7:12-17).

The prophetic voice. After David, the Israelites tended to associate the kingdom hope with the nation. The prophets, particularly Amos, spoke to them about this false identification. God's purposes were not to be fulfilled through any earthly state, the prophets said. On the contrary, all nations and societies stand under the judgment of God. In particular, Amos and the other prophets point to the judgment of God against the nation of Israel. Israel has broken the covenant with God through its unfaithfulness. It has not been obedient to its agreement. It has gone after false gods. It has sought material wealth and luxury while tolerating immorality, overlooking poverty, and remaining indifferent to justice. For that reason God is bringing Israel to judgment. Through this message the prophets succeed in separating the kingdom hope from the nation. The hope of Israel lies apart from national hope.

The new covenant. The hope of Israel, according to Jeremiah, lies in a new covenant. This new covenant will not be an external one. Rather, it will be written on the heart. National ruin is not the end, for God will create a spiritual Israel, a people of a new heart. They will be obedient to God because His law will be written on their hearts (Jer. 31:31-34).

The hope of a new Israel. This hope of a new Israel becomes even clearer in the writings of Isaiah. He says that the new Israel will be more glorious than the former one. God will establish a people under His rule. History, according to Isaiah, is moving in the direction of establishing this new Israel. This new domain will extend over the whole earth and include all the people who turn to God. It will be a time of peace and prosperity, a time when God's reign will extend throughout the world (Isa. 40–66).

The suffering servant. In the midst of this tremendous hope that a new Israel will fill the earth and be triumphant over all its enemies, Isaiah introduces a new concept, the idea of the suffering servant. This servant is the one through whom the victory of the people of God will be accomplished, the means through which God will establish His kingdom. But the servant is to suffer, to make his life a sin-offering to others—for it is through his suffering that his mission is accomplished (Isa. 42:1-7; 49:1-6; 50:1-9; 52–53; 61:1-3, 6-7).

The apocalyptic hope. This hope, found chiefly in Daniel, is that God will finally establish His kingdom over the whole world in the end time. It expresses the longing that God will conquer all His foes and rule victoriously over all. Its emphasis is that God will do what man has been unable to do. God's kingdom in the end is not man's creation but God's. And it is accomplished through the Son of Man

Having surveyed the ideas implicit in the idea of the kingdom in the Old Testament, we are prepared to turn to the New Testament to examine Jesus' understanding of Himself in relation to the hope of Israel. Jesus' understanding of the kingdom is our key to both the Old Testament view of the kingdom and the relation between the kingdom and the church. When we have grasped this, we will be in a better position to understand the role of the Christian in culture.

THE KINGDOM OF GOD AND JESUS

Jesus' self-understanding cannot be separated from His saturation in the Old Testament. Christian tradition has always affirmed that the Old and New Testaments are one book, not two. Consequently, we must never treat lightly the connection between the two Testaments. In the case of Jesus and the kingdom, we may see the relation between the two Testaments in two ways: (1) the kingdom expectation and Jesus, and (2) Jesus, Satan, and the kingdom.

The kingdom expectation and Jesus

Since the time of the exile, Jewish anticipation of the kingdom was running high. This hope for the kingdom, born out of the Old Testament experience of longing for God's reign on earth, explains the positive response given to John the Baptist when he came preaching "Repent, for the kingdom of heaven is at hand" (Matt. 3:2). John's message for Israel was that God was about to act, that God would visit His people in judgment and salvation.

When Jesus came to John for his baptism, both Jesus and John recognized their relation to each other in the coming of the kingdom. Although John did not *fully* understand Jesus' relation to the kingdom, he understood enough to recognize Jesus as the coming one. And Jesus understood Himself to be the one who had come "to fulfill all righteousness" (Matt. 3:15).

Although Jesus' message about the kingdom is the same as John's—"Repent, for the kingdom of Heaven is at hand" (Matt. 4:17)—there is a fundamental difference between the two: John proclaimed the *coming* of the kingdom, while Jesus proclaimed the *actualization* of the kingdom.[4]

This note of fulfillment is the distinguishing feature of Jesus' proclamation of the kingdom. When He came to his hometown of Nazareth He declared: "The Spirit of the Lord is upon me, because he has anointed me to preach good news to the poor. He has sent me to proclaim release to the captives and recovering of sight to the blind, to set at liberty those who are oppressed, to proclaim the acceptable year of the Lord" (Luke 4:18-19). That Jesus considered this an event that was happening is evident in His statement that "today this scripture has been fulfilled in your hearing" (Luke 4:21). (Note the cultural implications of Luke 4:18-19, quoted above.)

The unprecedented point that Jesus was making was that the kingdom was here and was actually taking place before their eyes.[5] But the record states that they did not receive Jesus and His message; they "rose up and put him out of the city, and led him to the brow of the hill on which their city was built, that they might throw him down headlong" (Luke 4:29). Why?

The reason why Jesus was not received by the Jews was

that He did not fulfill their expectations of the messianic kingdom. They wanted a Messiah who would lead the struggle for
independence from Rome. They were looking for an earthly
kingdom, a restoration of the Davidic ideal. But Jesus never
spoke of reestablishing the Davidic kingdom, nor did He set
Himself forth in any way as a political leader. Those who were
living by an apocalyptic hope expected the Messiah to come in
the clouds of heaven to destroy all His enemies and set up His
kingdom. Even though Jesus referred to Himself as the Son of
man, He never did what the Son of man was expected to
do—He did not open the heavens to destroy all His adver-
saries.

Furthermore, they expected the Messiah to be a new
Moses (Deut. 18:15-19), and many of Jesus' followers hailed
Him as this. He presented His teachings on the mountain as
Moses did. On the other hand, He didn't keep the Sabbath
strictly, He wasn't always concerned with ceremonial cleanli-
ness, and He kept the worst company. But even more serious
than those problems was His claim to be divine. For Judaism
this was an intolerable claim. After all, Jesus was the son of a
carpenter. What right did He have to regard Himself as
standing in such an intimate relationship with God? For this
the Jews had only one answer: "We have a law, and by that
law he ought to die, because he has made himself the Son of
God" (John 19:7).

The fact is that Jesus *did* fulfill the Old Testament expectation. But that expectation had been so defaced in the years
between the Old and the New Testament that it was barely
recognizable. Only after the death and resurrection of Christ
did the church recognize that Jesus was from the line of David
(Acts 2:25-36); that He was the inaugurator of a new age (Acts
2:17-21); that *He* was the New Covenant (Heb. 7-10); and
that through Him a new Israel had been born (1 Peter 2:9-10).
What Israel missed was the central motif of Jesus' entire
preaching and ministry—that the Messiah was the Suffering
Servant. Their expectations were external and had to do with
worldly power, a visible king, the rule of Jerusalem over the

world, strength, and military might. In all of this Jesus was a disappointment.

Jesus, Satan, and the Kingdom

The second point concerning Jesus and the kingdom that we need to know about in order to understand the role of the Christian in culture is the conflict that exists between Satan and Jesus.[6] This conflict goes all the way back to the Fall and is first introduced in Genesis 3:15—"I will put enmity between you and the woman, and between your seed and her seed; he shall bruise your head, and you shall bruise his heel."

Both the Old and the New Testament recognize the cosmic struggle between good and evil, light and darkness. But this struggle assumes clearer shape in the New Testament, where it is recognized as a struggle between two kingdoms—the kingdom of Satan and the kingdom of Christ. The New Testament is a witness to the victory of Christ and His kingdom over Satan. This concept is central not only to the whole Christian understanding of redemption but also to the entire question of the Christian's relation to the world.

The point is that Satan has been defeated. This comes up at several crucial points in the New Testament. First, there is Jesus' own statement about it in Matthew 12. He has been casting out demons, much to the consternation of the Pharisees. They chide Him, saying, "It is only by Be-elzebul, the prince of demons, that this man casts out demons" (Matt. 12:24). Jesus' answer communicates several levels of meaning. On the one hand He affirms the presence of the kingdom of God by saying, "If it is by the Spirit of God that I cast out demons, then the kingdom of God has come upon you" (Matt. 12:28). On the other hand, He indicated that the presence of His kingdom, evidenced by His power to cast out devils, presupposed the defeat of Satan's kingdom, for "how can one enter a strong man's house and plunder his goods, unless he first binds the strong man?" (Matt. 12:29).

But where did this defeat of Satan take place? According to the New Testament, we are warranted in looking at three events for an answer to this question: the Temptation, the Cross, and the Second Coming.

The temptation of Jesus by Satan is crucial. The crux of it is Satan's offering to Jesus all the kingdoms of the world. The issue for Jesus is not moral but messianic. Satan's temptation is a subtle way of offering Jesus the right to rule over the kingdoms of the world without suffering. When Jesus chooses obedience to the will of God over Satan, He reverses the choice of disobedience made by Adam. The power to rule over the world will come by obedience to the Father. This is why Jesus' rejection of the temptation is already the beginning of His victory over Satan. It represents the *presence* and the *power* of the kingdom of God. It is the point at which Jesus enters the strong man's house and binds him. The casting out of demons, therefore, is a demonstration of the power of Jesus and His kingdom over the power of Satan and his kingdom.

The second demonstration of the power of Christ's kingdom over Satan is at the Cross. Here Jesus, as Paul states, "disarmed the principalities and powers and made a public example of them, triumphing over them in him" (Col. 2:15). The Cross is crucial, for through the Cross all the power of Satan and evil is potentially destroyed. The Resurrection points to the defeat of sin and death; as Paul writes, "Death is swallowed up in victory. O death, where is thy victory? O death, where is thy sting? The sting of death is sin, and the power of sin is the law. But thanks be to God, who gives us the victory through our Lord Jesus Christ" (1 Cor. 15:55-57). What happened on the Cross was a reversal of the Fall. At the Fall the first Adam brought sin, death, and condemnation. At the Cross the second Adam brought righteousness, life, and justification (Rom. 5:12-21). Therefore, "as in Adam all die, so also in Christ shall all be made alive" (1 Cor. 15:22). In the death of Christ the final ruin and end of the city of man is certain—just as in His death the birth of the city of God begins to take shape. The kingdom of God is no longer future. It has become a *present* reality in the world.

The third portrayal of Christ's power over the kingdom of

Satan lies in the future and is expressed in the New Testament apocalyptic literature. In this picture the kingdom of Satan is finally destroyed and put away forever. There appear to be two stages in this final destruction of Satan. The first takes place after the Second Coming and before the beginning of the Millennium. Satan is "seized" and "bound for a thousand years" so that "he should deceive the nations no more" (Rev. 20:2-3). After the thousand years (during which Christ rules in His kingdom over the earth), Satan is released, and a final great battle takes place between the kingdom of Christ and the kingdom of Satan. Satan is defeated and "Death and Hades" are "thrown into the lake of fire" (Rev. 20:14).

The kingdom of God is both present and future. The rule of God is here and now in the world in those who are obedient to Christ. But the total rule of God through Christ is yet to come.[7]

We are now at the point where we can begin to draw from the kingdom idea its implications for the Christian in culture. We have already seen that the notion of "God's rule" is at the heart of biblical faith. Both in the Old Testament and in the New, God calls forth a people *to be obedient to Him in all areas of life.* Such a calling naturally has cultural implications. Whenever people are not obedient to God, their disobedience is expressed in their unfolding of culture; whenever people are obedient to God, their obedience is likewise expressed in their unfolding of culture. For this reason there are always two cities present in the world, the city of man and the city of God. These two cities are the earthly manifestation of the cosmic struggle taking place between the kingdom of Satan and the kingdom of Christ.

In the Old Testament God has been working with a historical people on two levels. On one level they are the people through whom the ultimate defeat of Satan is to come, for out of their midst the King comes to defeat and destroy the power of the evil one. On another level these people are called to live in obedience to God in every aspect of their lives—moral, social, political, and religious. Their obedience or disobedience is always, as we have seen, reflected in a cultural way.

Now the question we must ask, one that is crucial to our understanding of the role of the Christian in culture, is this: How, if at all, does the situation of "God's people under his rule" change in New Testament times?

THE KINGDOM OF GOD AND THE CHURCH

Although there is a continuity between the people of God in the Old Testament and in the New, there is also a difference, because in the New the redemption has taken place, the kingdom has come. We will examine this difference under three headings: the cosmic redemption, the true Israel, and kingdom ethics and the church.

The Cosmic Redemption

The first fact to keep in mind about the coming, death, and resurrection of Christ is that the cosmic redemption has occurred. Behind this idea of a cosmic redemption is the recognition that man *and the earth* are God's creation and that what happens to man affects the earth.[8] This principle is seen first in the garden. The earth was affected by man's sin. God said, "Cursed is the ground because of you" (Gen. 3:17). When Cain sinned against God by destroying his brother, God again set forth the relation between man and the earth, saying, "Now you are cursed from the ground" (Gen. 4:11). The relation between the earth and redemption is also expressed in the eschatological hope of Israel. Isaiah stressed the transformation of nature (Isa. 40–66) and lived in the hope that a new earth would replace the old one: "For behold, I create new heavens and a new earth; and the former things shall not be remembered or come into mind" (Isa. 65:17).

The New Testament writers frequently point to the dissolution of the old earth and the creation of a new one. Paul informs us (Romans 8) that the present creation "waits with eager longing for the revealing of the sons of God." This creation, which was "subjected to futility," will some day "be set free from its bondage to decay and obtain the glorious liberty of the children of God." In the meantime "the whole creation has been groaning in travail together until now." Mankind is also included in this longing, for Paul writes that "not only the creation, but we ourselves, who have the first fruits of the Spirit, groan inwardly as we wait for adoption as sons, the redemption of our bodies" (Rom. 8:19-25). This eschatological hope belongs not only to human beings but to the whole Creation. It is the longing to return to the original perfection, an attribute that will characterize the whole created order in the new heavens and the earth. (See 2 Peter 3:11-13; Revelation 12–22.)

The implication of cosmic redemption for the church is that the church is not merely a spiritual entity, having to do only with "spiritual" things like worship, prayer, and preaching; by virtue of the redemption in which it participates, it belongs to this earth and participates in the hope for newness that permeates all the structures of the created order.

The True Israel

The second fact to keep in mind about the coming, death, and resurrection of Christ is that a *new* people has been called into being to live under God's rule. Peter wrote to the believers, "Once you were no people but now you are God's people; once you had not received mercy but now you have received mercy" (1 Peter 2:10). These people, who constitute the New Testament church, are described in the same terms that were used to describe God's people in the Old Testament: they are "a chosen race, a royal priesthood, a holy nation, God's own people" (1 Peter 2:9).

The real point is that God has a *people* called to be obedient to His will, to live under His rule.[9] In the Old Testament these people have a particular identity with Israel. But not all people who belong to Israel are God's people. Jeremiah brings this out clearly. Only an obedient people can remain in true covenant with God, for He rules over only the obedient. The covenant bond is not merely external; it is of the heart (Jer. 4:3-4; cf. Deut. 10:16). Paul sets this forth quite clearly in

Romans: "For he is not a real Jew who is one outwardly, nor is true circumcision something external and physical. He is a Jew who is one inwardly, and real circumcision is a matter of the heart, spiritual and not literal" (2:28-29).

The spiritual nature of God's people points to the fact that the difference between His Old Testament people and His New Testament people is found not in the supposed dichotomy of Israel and the church but in the relation of the kingdom of God to the people of God. In the Old Testament the people of God anticipated the kingdom. In the New Testament the people of God witness to the kingdom, serve as the instrument of the kingdom, and act as the custodian of the kingdom.[10]

In both instances, in the Old and the New Testament, the people of God are *not* identifiable with the kingdom of God. The kingdom is the reign or rule of God. Consequently, as George Eldon Ladd puts it, "The Kingdom is not identified with its subjects. They are the people of God's rule who enter it, live under it, and are governed by it."[11] The difference, then, between Israel and the church is that the kingdom of God is no longer active through Israel. Says Ladd: "The Kingdom of God, as the redemptive activity and rule of God in Christ, created the church and works through the church in the world."[12] The church is therefore the instrument of the kingdom between the Cross and the Second Coming. It stands between the presence of the kingdom (now) and the future of the kingdom (not yet).

Kingdom Ethics and the Church

We have seen that the life, death, and resurrection of Christ establish Christ as God's King. We have also seen that His kingdom extends over the whole world, because His redemptive activity affects the earth as well as man. And within this world He has a called-out people (the church) who witness to His kingdom as both present and future.

Since the kingdom of God in its eschatological form is the rule of God over a perfect creation, and since this kingdom is now present because of redemption, the whole question of personal and social ethics is raised. To what extent is the perfection of the future kingdom to be realized in the present world order?[13]

Before finding an answer to this question, we must first identify kingdom ethics. The total ethical teaching of Jesus may be regarded as kingdom ethics. Most of this teaching is summarized in the Sermon on the Mount.

It is generally accepted that Jesus' ethics are absolute. That is, they are not ethics for a few, not ethics for a particular time (the Millennium), but ethics for the present and for all. Jesus fully expected His disciples to keep His teaching, and the same demand is made of the church. To quote Ladd again, Jesus' ethics "portray the ideal of the man in whose life the reign of God is absolutely realized."[14] Even though these ethics can be *perfectly* followed only in the eschatological state, they can be attained to a certain degree in this world.

That they are ethics for this world is clearly seen in the structure of life they presuppose. They assume evil, such as anger, murder, lust, hypocrisy, and materialism. In the eschatological kingdom none of these will be present. It will be a perfect order, without evil.

Another question is whether Jesus' ethics are meant only for the individual or whether He is setting forth a social ethic for the church as well. Since the church is the *body* of Christ in a collective and not merely individual sense, it would seem that Jesus' ethics are for the whole community. This does not mean that the church is to act as a political institution in the world: it is to function as "salt" and "light" (Matt. 5:13-14).

A second reason why Jesus' ethics seem to be meant as a social ethic lies in the nature of the kingdom itself. Because the redemption is cosmic, affecting man *and* the earth, and because the victory over evil has already been accomplished by Jesus on the Cross, it follows that the presence of the kingdom brings with it an invasion against all evil wherever it may be found. Since evil is both personal and, through the personal, social, most people who are called to witness to the kingdom and act as the instruments of the kingdom have the responsibility of living in such a way that they both expose evil and promote righteousness.

This argument for a social ethic arising out of the kingdom in no way supports a naive utopianism. The kingdom is made a reality not by men but by God, and then only at the consummation of history, when Christ comes to defeat the powers of evil and establish His kingdom.

CONCLUSION

We are now in a position to look back over the argument of this chapter and develop some basic principles. We want to understand how the kingdom relates to the role of the Christian in culture.

Let me suggest these principles as basic to our concern:

1. The idea of the kingdom is the rule of God over His people and His creation.

2. There is a "people of God" in both the Old Testament and the New Testament who are the people of the kingdom.

3. In the Old Testament the "people of God" anticipate the coming kingdom. Christ inaugurates the kingdom and points to the eschatological state when the kingdom will be fulfilled.

4. The church is a witness to and an instrument of the kingdom.

5. The responsibility of the church is to make the future kingdom present in the world insofar as is possible.

It is my contention that the church in history has attempted to fulfill its responsibility to the kingdom in this world by seeking to be the kingdom in three ways: (1) apart from the world, (2) through the world, and (3) by converting the world. I call these the separational, identificational, and transformational models. We turn now to the history of the church and to an examination of these models of kingdom responsibility.

Questions for Discussion

1. Scan the chapter and write down all those words and terms that are unfamiliar to you. Define them in your own words. What do these ideas have to do with the Christian in culture?
2. How is the idea of Christ's death as a "victory over the rule of Satan" central in the issues of the Christian's relationship to the world?
3. The church as the "body" of Christ is called to extend the victory of Christ over evil in the world. State some ways the church can express her power over evil in the world today. What has you church done?

Further Reading

Bright, John. *The Kingdom of God*. Nashville: Abingdon, 1953.
Ladd, George Eldon. *Crucial Questions About the Kingdom*. Grand Rapids: Eerdmans, 1952.
——. *The Gospel of the Kingdom*. Grand Rapids: Eerdmans, 1961.
——. *The Presence of the Future*. Grand Rapids: Eerdmans, 1974.
Pannenberg, Wolfhart. *Theology and the Kingdom*. Philadelphia: Westminster, 1966.
Perrin, Norman. *The Kingdom of God in the Teaching of Jesus*. London: SCM, 1963.
Ridderbos, Herman. *The Coming of the Kingdom*. Philadelphia: Presbyterian and Reformed, 1962.

HISTORICAL
BACKGROUND

5

The Separational Model

The problem of the Christian in culture is rooted, as we have seen, in the tension created by living in two worlds simultaneously. The Christian lives both in the world and in the kingdom.

The separational model of the Christian in culture emphasizes both the necessity that the Christian live by the kingdom of God quite apart from an involvement in the world and his ability to do so. The *necessity* of living by the kingdom of God is grounded in the antithesis that exists between the kingdom of God and the kingdom of evil. They are two wholly distinct spheres of life. The *ability* of the Christian to live in one sphere and not the other resides in his power of choice. "Choose ye this day whom ye will serve," "Come out from among them and be ye separate"—these are not to be regarded as mere word games. They describe actual choices that the Christian must make. The separation from the kingdom of evil is ultimately a matter of Christian obedience.

THE BIBLICAL BASIS

The separatists believe that the Bible abounds in examples of this kind of radical obedience. For example, Noah was chosen to build an ark for eight people in the midst of a culture so wicked "that every imagination of the thoughts of [man's] heart was only evil continually" (Gen. 6:5). Abraham was called *out* of his country to establish a new people: "Go from your country and your kindred and your father's house to the land that I will show you" (Gen. 12:1). Abraham had no attachment to the city of man, for "he sojourned in the land of promise, as in a foreign land" and "looked forward to the city which has foundations, whose builder and maker is God" (Heb. 11:9-10). Likewise Moses refused to be identified with the Egyptians who reared him, "choosing rather to share ill-treatment with the people of God than to enjoy the fleeting pleasures of sin" (Heb. 11:25). The same is true of the prophets: "They were stoned, they were sawn in two, they were killed with the sword; they went about in skins of sheep and goats, destitute, afflicted, ill-treated—of whom the world was not worthy—wandering over deserts and mountains, and in dens and caves of the earth" (Heb. 11:37-38). What all these people have in common is that they separated themselves from the culture of one world.

This theme, that Christians are to be separate from the world, is regarded by the separatists as the explicit teaching of Jesus and the disciples. They believe that Jesus' teaching in the Sermon on the Mount supports the idea of an antithesis between the followers of Christ and the world. Jesus stated that "no one can serve two masters; for either he will hate the one and love the other, or he will be devoted to the one and despise the other. You cannot serve God and mammon" (Matt. 6:24). Furthermore, Peter described the Christian community as "aliens and exiles" (1 Peter 2:11), and John supported the antithesis by admonishing Christians not to "love the world or the things in the world. If anyone loves the world, love for the Father is not in him. For all that is in the world, the lust of the flesh and the lust of the eyes and the pride of life, is not of the Father but is of the world. And the world passes away, and the lust of it; but he who does the will of God abides forever" (1 John 2:15). This attitude, as directed against the state, is particularly evident in Revelation, where John sees Rome as "the beast."

Finally, separation from the world, according to the separatist, is grounded in a proper understanding of the two kingdoms. The separatist maintains that the two are so radically different that one can live in one or the other but not both at the same time. This is the doctrine of the "radical antithesis." It assumes that sin has permeated every area of the world to such an extent that the true Christian cannot traffic with the world without compromising with sin and becoming contaminated by it. The church is therefore a counterculture, a culture within the culture, which lives by kingdom principles and values. The church is a pilgrim-people, sojourners whose citizenship is above. Any attachment to this world—to its goals, its pleasures, its wealth—must be denied for the sake of the kingdom of God.[1]

With these preliminary biblical and theological arguments in mind, we turn to the history of the church to find some examples of the separational model. The three most prominent examples are the pre-Constantinian church, the Anabaptists, and the contemporary communal movement.

THE PRE-CONSTANTINIAN CHURCH

During the first three centuries of the church, it was quite obvious to the Christian that life consisted of living in two worlds simultaneously. Church and state were antithetical to each other. The phenomenon of the state against the church doubtless had much to do with the church's separational stance.[2]

The Roman State Against the Church

The Roman state dominated the religions of the empire. This was quite natural, since the purpose of religion was to serve the state. That is, it was believed that as long as the gods were pleased with the worship of the people, they would bless the Roman Empire. Consequently, the Romans attributed the peace and prosperity of their empire to the gods and encouraged their people to be religious.

Since religion was in the hands of the Roman senate, only those gods that had been approved by the senate could be worshiped. Nevertheless, as the empire expanded and people from all over the Mediterranean moved to Rome, the quantity and diversity of religions increased greatly. In order to give some kind of unity to all these religions, the Romans instituted a new cult centered in the person of the emperor. Everyone was required to recognize the emperor. Although the emperor was regarded as "deity," he was not considered a god. "Deity" was defined as "the giver of good things." The Romans were to give honor and praise to the emperor as the *symbol* of the gods who gave prosperity to Rome and made it great. Consequently, the names of most of the traditional gods of Rome were attached to the emperor cult.

The circumstances, then, in which Christianity was born and grew were rather difficult. The state was in itself a religion. And in order to participate in the state one needed to recognize its religious character, especially as symbolized in the emperor. This the Christian could not do. The natural result was an increasing tension between church and state.[3]

Several factors heightened the tension between church and state. For one thing, Christianity began as a Jewish movement. Since the Jews were already out of favor with the Romans, it was natural to transfer hatred from the Jew to Jewish Christians. Furthermore, like the Jews, the Christians were unable to produce an image of their God, and, like the Jews, they denied the existence of all gods except their own. The Romans concluded from this that Christians were "atheists." Furthermore, it was rumored that Christian worship consisted of some form of cannibalism. They ate the "body" and the "blood" of the "Son." The gossip in Rome was that Christians met in secret, butchered babies, ate their flesh, drank their blood, and ended their meeting with orgies.

The Romans concluded from this that Christians were immoral. Another severe problem was related to the Christians' anticipation of the coming kingdom of Christ and His rule over the world. Their apocalyptic hopes anticipated the destruction of all empires, the downfall of Rome, and the setting up of Christ's kingdom. News of this sort struck fear into the hearts of the Roman rulers and caused the Romans to look on Christians as political anarchists. These attitudes show that the Christians hardly had a chance with the Roman state. Without a chance to receive a hearing they were judged to be atheists, immoralists, and political anarchists.

Persecution against the Christians began in the first century under Nero and by the turn of the century had spread to other parts of the Roman Empire. But the persecutions were sporadic and local until the third century. Then several factors came into play to prompt a more systematic attempt to rid the empire of the Christians. For one thing, the fortunes of the empire were at low tide. Since the worship of the gods was regarded as integral to the continued prosperity of the state, it was thought that the gods were displeased and that their displeasure was expressed in the declining prosperity and stability of the Roman Empire. The widespread popularity of Christianity among the people made it suspect. Perhaps the gods were unhappy with the negative influence of these atheistic, immoral persons. Given these conditions and the fact that Christians supported the coming kingdom of Christ, the intensified persecution against them is understandable.

The Attitude of the Church Toward the State

The development of the church's attitude toward the state was related to the church's eschatology. It was the general consensus that the present world order would be completely destroyed by fire in the end time. In this sense the early church was informed by the vision of Peter, that of "waiting for and hastening the coming of the day of God, because of which the heavens will be kindled and dissolved, and the elements will melt with fire!" (2 Peter 3:12). But the church also

looked forward to a restored paradise. In the tradition of
Paul's teaching, the believers anticipated that "the creation
itself will be set free from its bondage to decay and obtain the
glorious liberty of the children of God" (Rom. 8:21). Irenaeus
summed up the consensus that it was neither the substance
nor the essence of creation that would pass away but the
fashion of the world. "But when this [present] fashion [of
things] passes away, and man has been renewed, and
flourishes in an incorruptible state, so as to preclude the possibility of becoming old, [then] there shall be the new heaven
and the new earth, in which the new man shall remain, always
holding fresh converse with God."[4] This eschatological vision,
coupled with a strong conviction that Christ's return was in
the near future, fixed the vision of a perfect society in the
future. The idea that the perfect kingdom of God could be
realized on earth was quite foreign to the ancient Christian
mind.

Nevertheless, Christian loyalty to the vision of the future
kingdom of God did not mean that Christians were anarchists
or disloyal to the state. The Fathers made it very clear that
Christians did not have the right to rebel against the government. Christians, according to Justin, were taught civil obedience by Christ and were therefore to be accounted among the
best citizens. "And everywhere we, more readily than all men,
endeavor to pay to those appointed by you the taxes both
ordinary and extraordinary."[5] Therefore, Justin continued,
"to God alone we render worship, but in other things we
gladly serve you, acknowledging you as kings and rulers of
men, and praying that with your kingly power you be found to
possess also sound judgment."[6] Likewise, Tertullian made it
clear that Christians refused to worship the emperor because
he was not God but that Christians were nevertheless loyal to
the emperor.

The charge that Christians were immoral was also re-
futed with the assertion that the morality of Christians
strengthened the fabric of Roman society. Theophilus, in his
"Letter to Autolycus," reminded him that with the Christians

"temperance dwells, self-restraint is practiced, monogamy is observed, chastity is guarded, iniquity exterminated, sin extirpated, righteousness exercised, law administered, worship performed, God acknowledged."[7] The philosopher Aristides wrote that "they do not commit adultery nor fornication, nor bear false witness, nor covet the things of others. . . . They are eager to do good to their enemies; they are gentle and easy to be entreated. . . . [They] live holy and just lives, as the Lord enjoined upon them."[8]

Although the early Christians were unwilling to participate in the government, they nevertheless believed that it functioned by divine sanction. They stood in the tradition of Paul, who wrote that "every person" should be "subject to the governing authorities" (Rom. 13:1), and of Peter, who likewise insisted that Christians "be subject for the Lord's sake to every human institution, whether it be to the emperor as supreme, or to governors as sent by him to punish those who do wrong and to praise those who do right" (1 Peter 2:13-14).

Irenaeus summed up the general attitude in his work *Against Heresies.* He wrote that it was God who has "appointed the Kingdoms of this world" and that "God imposed upon mankind the fear of man, as they did not acknowledge the fear of God, in order that, being subjected to the authority of men, and kept under restraint by their laws, they might attain to some degree of justice, and exercise mutual forbearance through dread of the sword."[9]

Although the government has a divine function, the early Christians nevertheless looked on government as a "human institution." Government was instituted as a result of the Fall. Consequently, it would not be needed in the new heavens and the new earth. The important feature of this conviction is that the early Christians did not assume that the government could become Christian. For that reason they "looked forward to the city which has foundations, whose builder and maker is God" (Heb. 11:10).

Naturally, this eschatological vision of the future kingdom affected their way of life. The anonymous author of the *Letter to Diognetus* summarized their place in the world in this way:

> Christians cannot be distinguished from the rest of the human race by country or language or customs. They do not live in cities of their own; they do not use a peculiar form of speech; they do not follow an eccentric manner of life. . . . They live in their own countries, but only as aliens. They have a share in everything as citizens, and endure everything as foreigners. . . . They busy themselves on earth, but their citizenship is in heaven.[10]

Christians in Society

From the very beginnings of the church, Christians recognized that they were part of society but that they were to be *different*. In the *Didache*, the earliest Christian manual, the text begins by saying, "There are two ways, one of life and one of death; and between the two ways there is a great difference."[11] There follows a detailed description of how the Christian is to live, what he is to do and what he is to refrain from doing. These prescriptions are most revealing because they show that Christian obedience must take shape in respect to society and societal norms. This document is only one of many that give us insight into Christian living. Let us look briefly at some of the major concerns of these early documents.

In the first place, Christians generally refused to be involved in the state government. We do know that government officials and workers in the New Testament period became Christians and apparently stayed in these positions.[12] But by the end of the second century, involvement in the military and civil service was avoided. Hippolytus, for example, indicates that a person who is in military service and becomes a Christian may remain, but "if a catechumen or a believer seeks to become a soldier, they must be rejected, for they have despised God."[13] A similar attitude was taken toward civil service. Hippolytus insists that a "civic magistrate that wears the purple must resign or be rejected" (from the church).[14] (Judges were continually called on to pronounce and inflict capital punishment. They were also involved in the support of emperor-worship.) Tertullian summarized the attitude of the early church by insisting that "there is no agreement between the divine and the human sacrament [the word here means oath], the standard of Christ and the standard of the devil, the camp of light and the camp of darkness. One soul cannot be due to two *masters*—God and Caesar."[15]

The early Christians also took a very negative view of Roman entertainment. Again, Hippolytus gives evidence of this in the screening of those who desire to become catechumens (converts in preparation for baptism and full membership in the church). He wrote that actors, charioteers, gladiators, or a person involved in any way with gladiatorial exhibitions must "desist or be rejected." Tertullian warned against shows in his work *On Shows*. After describing the permeation of idolatry in the circus and other show places, he insists that "we lapse from God . . . by touching and tainting ourselves with the world's sins." For that reason a Christian makes a break with his Maker by "going as a spectator to the circus and theatre," for "the polluted things pollute us."[16] Athenagoras warns against the shows because "to see a man put to death is much the same as killing him."[17]

The attitude of early Christians toward society was only partly negative. In many other ways they exerted a strong positive impact on society by their concern for upright living. Even a pagan critic like Lucian observed, "It is incredible to see the ardor with which the people of that religion help each other in their wants. They spare nothing. Their first legislator [Jesus] has put into their heads that they are all brethren."[18]

To begin with, Christians were willing to share their wealth. Their attitude toward possessions evidenced itself in Jerusalem, where "no one said that any of the things which he possessed was his own, but they had everything in common. . . . There was not a needy person among them, for as many as were possessors of lands or houses sold them, and brought the proceeds of what was sold and laid it at the apostles' feet; and distribution was made to each as any had need" (Acts 4:32-35). This attitude continued in the early church.

While there is little evidence that the churches actually banded themselves together in shared economic communities, there is much evidence that they continued to care for the needs of the brethren. Justin Martyr wrote, "We who valued above all things the acquisition of wealth and possessions, now bring what we have into a common stock, and communicate to every one in need."[19] Indeed, Martin Hengel in his work *Property and Riches in the Early Church* argues that "this idea that private property is a root of human dissension goes through the social admonitions of the fathers of the early church like a scarlet thread. The struggle for individual possessions destroys the original good order of the world, as all had an equal share in God's gifts."[20] There is also evidence that each congregation had a common fund to which all contributed for the benefit of the needy.

This spirit of hospitality evidenced itself in the attitude taken toward the sick, the poor, and the homeless. The classical world had displayed very little concern for the needy. Plato, for example, thought that allowing the poor to die would shorten their misery. Ancient society even allowed orphans to be raised for prostitution. Christians, by contrast, were concerned about the poor, were active in hospitality to the stranger, and set about caring for orphans and castaway children. Aristides described this social awareness as follows:

> Falsehood is not found among them; and they love one another, and from widows they do not turn away their esteem; and they deliver the orphan from him who treats him harshly. And he who has gives to him who has not, without boasting. And when they see a stranger, they take him in to their homes and rejoice over him as a very brother; for they do not call them brethren after the flesh, but brethren after the spirit and in God. And whenever one of their poor passes from the world, each one of them according to his ability gives heed to him and carefully sees to his burial. And if they hear that one of their number is imprisoned or afflicted on account of the name of their Messiah, all of them anxiously minister to his necessity, and if it is possible to redeem him they set him free. And if there is among them any that is poor and needy, and if they have no spare food, they fast two or three days in order to supply the needy their lack of food.[21]

Christians also took a more humane approach toward slavery. Most slaves were originally captured soldiers whose owners had complete control over their lives. In the second century, a series of laws made conditions for slaves more tolerable. They were able to accumulate enough wealth to buy their own freedom. The evidence is that Christians also owned slaves but regarded them in a kindly way: Paul admonished Philemon to take Onesimus back not as a slave but as a beloved brother (Philem. 16). Aristides informs us that "if one or another of them have bondmen and bondwomen or children, through love towards them persuade them to become Christians, and when they have done so, they call them brethren without distinction."[22] We know that the church encouraged the release of slaves, that there was a liturgy for this, and that it was not infrequent for a slave-owner to set a number of slaves free on the day of his baptism. Christian slaves were also active in the church, and one of them, Collistus, became bishop of Rome in A.D. 220.

Christians also created a positive effect on society through their emphasis on morality and stable marriages. At a time when moral laxity was high and the family structure was breaking down, the Christian church insisted on high moral standards. As the author of the *Letter to Diognetus* said, "They marry, like everyone else. . . . They share their board with each other, but not their marriage bed."[23]

Conclusion

We conclude that broad groups of the early Christians were separatists. This does not mean, however, that they were not concerned about making an impact on culture. Indeed, the author of the *Letter to Diognetus* declared "that the soul is in the body, that Christians are in the world. The soul is dispersed through all the members of the body, and Christians are scattered through all the cities of the world. The soul dwells in the body, but does not belong to the body, and Christians dwell in the world, but do not belong to the world."[24] Nevertheless, the anonymous author argues, "the soul is shut up in the body, and yet itself holds the body together; while Christians are restrained in the world as in a prison, and yet themselves hold the world together."[25]

It is striking to notice that these early Christian separatists did not develop a systematic theology to support their separatism. While a set of beliefs may underlie their approach toward the world, no early theologian actually put it together in such a way as to develop a theological platform for separatism. This provides a striking difference with the Anabaptists of the sixteenth century, whose contribution, among other things, is to provide the church with a theology for separatism.

THE ANABAPTISTS

Only recently has the Anabaptist contribution to the church begun to be appreciated by mainline Protestants and Catholics. In the sixteenth century the Anabaptists were regarded as left-wing radicals, and the onus of this stayed with them for a long time. The negative attitude toward the Anabaptists originated with the Reformers and other defenders of the state-church Protestantism that the Anabaptists opposed, and information about the Anabaptists has been drawn mainly from these hostile sources. However, twentieth-century historical scholarship has moved behind the myth, and a more accurate view has emerged.

The word *anabaptist* itself does not give us a clear picture of these so-called left-wing radicals. It is a Latin derivative of the Greek *anabaptismos*, meaning "rebaptism," and it means "one who rebaptizes." The word was originally used by Luther and Zwingli to describe those Protestants who separated themselves from the state church. Baptism was important only in that it was a distinguishing mark between two approaches to church organization. Infant baptism was the mark of the state churches. It was a law of the state that all infants were to be baptized into the church. Adult baptism (or rebaptism in the case of those converts originally baptized as infants) was a mark of a church that refused to be controlled by the state. The Anabaptists advocated a "free church" position. They would not submit to state control. Baptism constituted an act of civil disobedience. The word *Anabaptist* is inadequate because it points only to the act of baptism itself, whereas the deeper cause of anger and frustration on the part of Luther and Zwingli and others who opposed them was really the issue of whether the church was independent of the state or not.

Franklin Littell in *The Anabaptist View of the Church* puts his finger on the real meaning of the term *Anabaptist:* "The anabaptists proper were those in the radical Reformation who gathered and disciplined a 'true church' (Rechte Kirche) upon the apostolic pattern as they understood it."[26] While the word was used rather broadly, the groups I have in mind in this discussion include only those at the center, the more moderate Anabaptists such as "the Swiss Brethren," the "Hutterite Brethren," and the "Mennonites."[27]

A concern for the restitution of the church was central to these "mainline Anabaptists." It is the key, not only to the heart of the Anabaptist movement, but also to the Anabaptist view of culture. And so we must look first at the Anabaptists' view of church history and their concern to restore the true church.

The Anabaptist View of Church History

The heart of the Anabaptists' view of the church is their desire to follow the New Testament pattern of the church, which is expressed in a kind of voluntarism. Littell calls this a "primitivism."[28] Their objective was to restore something old, to return to the pure, primitive, unspoiled church of a bygone age.

Actually a kind of primitivism was already in the air in the sixteenth century. Many felt that the turmoil and revolution of the times was symptomatic of a fall that had occurred in national affairs, in the church, and in the age. Consequently there was a longing for the past, for the restoration of a purer era. For the church, the past model was the New Testament era and the pre-Constantinian church. Erasmus, for example, pointed to gospel simplicity as a way to rejuvenate the faith and the church. But Erasmus never broke with the Catholic church. Zwingli, another student of the Bible and the early Fathers, called for a return to the New Testament and to Christ. But Zwingli never repudiated the church-state connections of the Swiss city-state. Unlike Erasmus or Zwingli, the early Anabaptist leaders were willing to carry out the logic of their convictions. They were willing to turn their back on the present—on the Catholic church and on the state-church establishment—to restore the past.

This interest inevitably led them to conclude that the present church had fallen. In general, the consensus was that the church had fallen during the time of Constantine, when Christianity was declared to be the state religion (A.D. 324). This event marked a turning point for the church. No longer independent, it began to turn to the state for support. The church had therefore been in a fallen condition ever since Constantine.

This attitude of the Anabaptists inevitably led them to find certain "marks" of the fallen church.[29] The most obvious mark was the union of church and state. Through this compromise the church ceased to be a voluntary association of believers; the state was able to use power and coercion as a means of bringing people into the church. This, the Anabaptists asserted, was a denial of the spiritual significance of the church. It made the church little more than another human institution. A second mark of the fallen church was seen in the wars conducted in the name of Christianity. Violence of any kind and under any condition was rejected as alien to the spirit of New Testament Christianity and that of the early church. That the church could carry the sword, take an oath of allegiance, and enforce political, economic, and religious control through the use of power was obviously wrong. Another mark of the fallenness of the church, in the eyes of the Anabaptists, was the dead formalism that characterized its life and worship. The Anabaptists argued that spiritual strength was found in the inward man, in the heart, and not in the pomp and circumstances of the mass. This concern for the external fostered another mark of the fallen church—the lust for ecclesiastical position and the power that went with it. This unseemly desire for achievement stood behind the rise of the hierarchy. And through the hierarchy, power was abused.

The Anabaptists' rejection of the present state of the church caused them to focus on the early church, where none of these marks were present. The early church was characterized instead by the separation of church and state, by a true inward spirituality, by a spirit of community and brotherhood, and by equality among Christians. The Anabaptists' desire to restore the early church led them into a view of eschatology that looked for the dissolution of the established church in the near future, the emergence of the inner church from it, and then an age of the persecution of the true church by the established church (the Antichrist). After this would come the return of Christ.

Underlying all these convictions is a basic theological conviction, the ardent belief in the two kingdoms.

The Anabaptist Doctrine of the Two Kingdoms

Even though the Anabaptists glorified the pre-Constantinian church, they were unlike the early Christians in one major respect: they had a well-worked-out theology of the kingdom.[30] This theology was rooted in a fundamental dualism that they found in the New Testament. It was, they believed, the major concern of Jesus to proclaim the presence of the kingdom. Entrance into the kingdom of Jesus was through a new birth, a radical reorientation in one's view of life and style of life in which one turned away from the sin of the world (the kingdom of evil) toward the values, virtues, and life style of Jesus. They took seriously the admonition of Paul that "we are not contending against flesh and blood, but against the principalities, against the powers, against the world rulers of this present darkness, against the spiritual hosts of wickedness in the heavenly places" (Eph. 6:12). They were unwilling to compromise with the world, to flirt with its passing fancies, or to be related to it in any way.

This concern to be separate from the world dominated the Schleitheim Confession of Faith,[31] a major Anabaptist statement written in 1527 by the Swiss Anabaptists. In the third article the authors state that "all those who have fellowship with the dead works of darkness have no part in the light" and that "all who follow the devil and the world have no part with those who are called unto God out of the world." The fourth article states that "all creatures are in but two classes, good and bad, believing and unbelieving, darkness and light, the world and those who (have come) out of the world, God's temple and idols, Christ and Belial; and none can have part with the other."

A more elaborate statement of the same idea is found in the anonymous *Great Article Book* of the Hutterites. This is generally regarded as having been written by Bishop Peter Walpot around 1577.[32]

Between the Christian and the world there exists a vast difference like that between heaven and earth. The world is the world, always remains the world, behaves like the world and all the world is nothing but world. The Christian, on the other hand, has been called away from the world. He has been called never to conform to the world, never to be a consort, never to run along with the crowd of the world and never to pull its yoke. The world lives according to the flesh and is dominated by the flesh. Those in the world think that no one sees what they are doing; hence the world needs the sword [of the authorities]. The Christians live according to the Spirit and are governed by the Spirit. They think that the Spirit sees what they are doing and that the Lord watches them. Hence they do not need and do not use the sword among themselves. The victory of the Christians is the faith that overcometh the world (I John 5:4), while the victory of the world is the sword by which they overcome [whatever is in their way]. To Christians an inner joy is given; it is the joy in their hearts that maintains the unity of the Spirit in the bond of peace (Ephesians 4:3). The world knows no true peace; therefore it has to maintain peace by the sword and force alone. The Christian is patient, as the apostle writes (I Peter 4:1): "As Christ hath suffered . . . arm yourself likewise with the same mind." The world arms itself for the sake of vengeance and (accordingly) strikes out with the sword. Among Christians he is the most genuine who is willing to suffer for the sake of God. The world, on the contrary, thinks him the most honorable who knows how to defend himself with the sword.

To sum up: friendship with the world is enmity with God. Whosoever, therefore, wishes to be a friend of the world makes himself an enemy of God (James 4:4). If to be a Christian would reside alone in words and an empty name, and if Christianity could be arranged as it pleases the world; if, furthermore, Christ would permit what is agreeable to the world, and the cross would have to be carried by a sword only . . . then both authorities and subjects—in fact, all the world—would be Christians. Inasmuch, however, as a man must be born anew (John 3:7), must die in baptism to his old life, and must rise again with Christ unto a new life and Christian conduct, such a thing cannot and shall not be: "It is easier," says Christ, "for a camel to go through the eye of a needle than for a rich man (by whom is meant here the authorities in particular) to enter the Kingdom of God or true Christianity" (Matthew 19:24).[33]

The striking feature of the Anabaptist theology of the kingdom is the absolute antithesis it sees between the kingdom of Christ and the kingdom of this world. As the *Great Article Book* points out, the kingdom of this world is "according to the flesh," "needs the sword," and "knows no true peace." On the other hand, the kingdom of Christ is "according to the Spirit" and "governed by the Spirit," and to it "an inner joy is given." The conclusion is reached that "whosoever, therefore, wishes to be a friend of the world makes himself an enemy of God."

This theology of the kingdoms and the view of the absolute antithesis between them lies at the heart of the Anabaptists' view both of the church and of the state. We cannot understand their view of Christians in culture without understanding this. We turn, then, to the implications of the antithesis between the two kingdoms and the Anabaptist view of the church and of the state.

The Anabaptist View of the Church

To begin with, it must be recognized that the Anabaptists would have nothing to do with the state-church concept prevalent in the sixteenth century. This was the main point in their separation from the Lutherans, the Zwinglians, and the Calvinists. The Anabaptists were all united in their conviction that the state church was a kind of culture-religion that had to be rejected before the true church (which was to have no connection with the culture of the world) could emerge.

This view forms the background for three Anabaptist convictions about the church. They believed that the church was a free association of believers, that it was a brotherhood of believers, and that the believers were characterized by radical obedience.

First and foremost, the Anabaptists regarded the church as a free association of believers. The institutional idea of the church to which people were admitted through baptism was, to them, a perversion of the New Testament ideal. They wished to restore the early church at Jerusalem as a community of Christians who had in common their new birth by the Holy Spirit and the desire to worship God in purity of spirit and simplicity. This concern, to have a free church, must not be confused with the modern notion of individualism wherein each person has a private experience of conversion and growth in Christ somewhat unrelated to that of the rest of the Christian community.

This brings us to their second conviction about the church, that it is a brotherhood of believers. The concept of brotherhood attempts to take seriously the idea of a visible community of believers into which the Christian enters and to which he is responsible. Likewise the community is responsible for each person. As Robert Friedmann describes it, "one cannot find salvation without caring for his brother. . . . It is not 'faith alone' which matters . . . but it is brotherhood, this intimate caring for each other, as it was commanded to the disciples of Christ as the way to God's Kingdom."[34] This concern for brotherhood is illustrated by the Anabaptist use of the "ban." Whenever a brother fell out of line with the Christian practice expected of him, he was banned from taking part in "the breaking of bread" as a method of punishment and correction.

The third conviction about the church was that it must be characterized by radical obedience. Once a believer has come to know God's will—through the Bible and in the community—there is nothing left for him to do except to obey. The Anabaptists looked on the commands of God as something to be taken literally and not merely spiritualized as Luther or Calvin would do. For example, the command to "forsake all" meant actually to forsake all and not merely to be *willing* to forsake all.

These three points illustrate the vast distance between the Anabaptists and the accepted state-church view of their time. It was the reason for which they suffered and the basis for their view of the state.

The Anabaptist View of the State

The first point, mentioned previously, is that the Anabaptists believed that the state belonged to the kingdom of this world. Therefore, because of the antithesis between the two kingdoms, the Anabaptists "acknowledged the primacy of the claims of God over the claims of government."[35]

This does not mean, however, that they did not recognize the state as a valid institution. Indeed, as the Schleitheim Confession states, "the sword is ordained of God outside the perfection of Christ. It punishes and puts to death the wicked, and guards and protects the good. In the law the sword was ordained for the punishment of the wicked and for their death, and the same [sword] is [now] ordained to be used by the worldly magistrates."[36] In this respect Romans 13 was used as the basis for all discussion about civil authority.

Consequently the Anabaptists insisted that Christians owed an obedience to the civil authorities as long as this obedience did not stand in the way of their primary commitment to God. They paid their taxes and followed the general customs required by the magistracy. In the beginning of the movement, when the government began to suppress it, the Anabaptists begged the government not to do so, sought official permission to publish their writings, asked for public hearing, petitioned for safe-conduct papers, and generally attempted to be obedient to Christ in a way that would be acceptable to the civil authorities. However, as they continued to be suppressed, they gradually had to move into civil disobedience on certain levels in order to remain obedient to their higher calling. They continued to meet and to preach despite the regulations against them. They refused to divulge the names of their brethren. They hid in the forests and mountains in an attempt to escape their persecutors, and they sometimes refused to surrender themselves to the court.[37]

Within this context it is easy to see that the Anabaptists would not support involvement in the state on any level. The Schleitheim Confession addresses three points in particular. First, "whether a Christian may or should employ the sword against the wicked for the defense and protection of the good." Second, "whether a Christian shall pass sentence in worldly disputes and strife such as unbelievers have with one another." And third, "Shall one be a magistrate if one should be chosen as such?" The argument in each case against involvement in the state is that "Christ did not. . . ; therefore we should do likewise." The point is that the government is according to the flesh but the Christian is according to the spirit. The Christian may be in this world, but his citizenship is in heaven, and therefore his allegiance belongs to Christ alone.[38]

This radical doctrine that underlies the Anabaptists' view of the church and state also determines their view of life in the world.

The Anabaptist Life in the World

In the first place, the Anabaptists had a strong sense of Christian discipleship. They insisted that there was a difference between reflection upon Christ and obedience to Christ. A major problem in the church, they thought, was that Christians spent too much time reflecting on Christ and not enough time imitating Christ. For them, the apostolic norm, to which all Christians were called, was an active, energetic attempt to be like Christ, to live as He did, to follow Him. For this reason the Sermon on the Mount was viewed as an expression of principles that were to be carried out in this world, in the here and now. It did not contain commands for a select few (monastics, for example), or teaching for a future age, or principles that were only for the inner man. As a consequence of this view, Anabaptists revolutionized the concept of monasticism and actually emerged with a view that all Christians were called into a kind of monastic life. The radical claims of Christianity were no longer for the few but for all. Such a radical view of discipleship had the effect of changing social structures for the Anabaptist community and, if accepted by all, had the potential of totally revolutionizing the structures of human society.[39]

This radical view of Christian discipleship caused the Anabaptists to be active in social service. They believed they were forerunners of the time when God would establish His kingdom on earth. This eschatological element was, therefore, a strong motivating factor in their witness to the world. They did not hope to save the present world so much as they lived in anticipation of the new order that God Himself would establish. Klassen, in his thorough treatment of this subject, wrote:

> The practice of mutual aid was considered a necessary and natural concomitant of spiritual fellowship. At secret meetings in cellars, fields, gardens, or forests, the persecuted groups would gather money, food, and clothing for those in need. Members were encouraged to place their gifts in the boxes and sacks provided for that purpose. . . . If the destitute were ill and unable to attend the meetings, their unfortunate circumstances were not forgotten.[40]

Another aspect of the Anabaptist life in the world was their insistence on nonresistance. "The Brethren understood this to mean complete abandonment of all warfare, strife, and violence, and of the taking of human life," comments Harold Bender.[41] It should be remembered that this life style was adopted at a time when the sword was being used in the name of religion for religious purposes. In this sense the Anabaptists were forerunners of those who hold to the modern concept of pacifism.[42]

A natural outcome of the doctrine of nonresistance was the insistence on religious liberty. This arose, says Bender, "not from any merely prudential, rationalistic, or ethical considerations, but from its central understanding of the nature of Christianity."[43] The Anabaptists believed that the conviction of Christianity came by the Holy Spirit and not by force. Therefore a person's conscience was not to be bound to the state but was to be free under God.

Conclusion

This brief analysis leads us to the firm conclusion that the Anabaptists belong to the separational model of Christians in culture. Christians were to create a culture within the culture. They were called to witness and to suffer in this world. For in them the kingdom of God had come and was taking shape in a hostile world. The Christian society was therefore to be built through the church, for this was where Christ reigned in the world.

This concept, which was first given distinctive shape among Protestants by the Anabaptists, has continued to appear in the history of the church. In Western Christianity it has appeared in what has become known as the community movement. We turn now to this movement as a modern expression of the separational view of the Christian in the world.

THE CHRISTIAN COMMUNITY MOVEMENT

The Christian community movement, particularly in America, cannot be understood apart from the cultural situation in the West. Over the past century and a half the Western way of life has drastically changed as a result of the industrial and technological revolutions. The industrial revolution turned raw materials into products and changed the Western way of life. It provided an economic stimulus that resulted in an unprecedented world of plenty. Then, as society became organized around technology, many aspects of the mechanized society had negative effects on human well-being;

among these were dehumanization, the growth of the "organization man," planned obsolescence, the loss of the dignity of work in mass production, and a deterioration of personal and family life. This situation, aggravated by the wars, poverty, hunger, and general chaos of the twentieth century, led to a spirit of pessimism and a deep questioning of society's values. It is in this context that the modern Christian communities have emerged.

There are many similarities between these communities and the pre-Constantine Christians as well as the Anabaptists. I will discuss only their distinctive marks. It should be noted, as a matter of interest, that these marks are largely pragmatic, arising out of the situation, and generally lacking a theological basis. They center around a concern for simple obedience to the radical demands of Jesus. And the communities take many forms, from some being loosely organized around fellowship and sharing to others being modeled on material and economic equality.[44]

To begin with, all of these communities are characterized by a concern for *radical obedience* that results in *community* and a *counterculture witness*.

Radical Obedience

One of the calls to community among evangelicals was made by Arthur Gish in his book *The New Left and Christian Radicalism*. In a chapter entitled "Compromise, Expedience and Obedience to Christ," he sets forth his understanding of what it means to be a follower of Christ: "To be a Christian is to be an extremist. Moderation is a Greek ideal, not Christian."[45]

The point is that radical Christianity centers in a literal and absolute obedience to Christ. It is an obedience not so much to principles or ideals as to a Person. Truth is relational and personal, not propositional (that is, not set down in statements that affirm or deny particular points). Therefore the heart of radical Christianity is not a system or an institution but a style of life, a style based squarely on the example of

Jesus. It is a determination to follow what He did and what He taught. The radical Christian is therefore freed from slavery to any human institution or to the expectation of others. He is free to be obedient to Christ, and therefore, to quote Gish again, "he does not make decisions on the basis of consequences, expediency, or effectiveness."[46] The reason this is true for the radical Christian is that his hopes are not in this world but in the vision of a new reality, namely, the kingdom of God. Although the full flowering of this kingdom is in the future, a form of it is in the world now, in the community of Christian people.

Community

Radical Christians look on the institutional church as secularized Christianity. It has succumbed to the ambitions of the world—numbers, power, prestige, wealth, comfort. Radical Christianity emphasizes Peter's description of the church as "aliens" (1 Peter 1:1). Christians are a pilgrim people, sojourners whose citizenship is in heaven. They are a set-apart people, called to live by a new standard within society.

Max Delespesse in his book *The Church Community* offers the following points about the church as a community:

1. *A perfect community.* The perfection of the community is not something it has in and of itself. It is a given. It arises out of two theological considerations: first, that the Christian community is the body of Christ (Eph. 5), and second, that it is indwelt by the power of the Holy Spirit.

2. *An all-embracing community.* The community of Christ is not merely a "spiritual" community as though that were the only reality. It embraces all of life. Therefore the divinity of Christ is to shine through human relationships in the church. This extends to the whole life of the Christian community, including the sharing of things. Because things are an extension of people, the sharing of things is a natural result of sharing in personal relationships.

3. *The church as community is a goal.* The church is the present reality of the eschatological hope. It is the community of

salvation. Salvation is present in the church because the church is already the final assembly of redeemed people. Therefore, as the church realizes the fruits of the Holy Spirit, it more and more expresses the final consummation of God's work in the world.

4. *The church as community for the salvation of the world.* The community of salvation exists not only for those who are within it but also for the salvation of all men. That is, the community points to, prepares, and calls others into the salvation offered by Christ to the whole world.[47]

It is from the commitment to radical obedience that community issues, and from community flows the counterculture witness.

The Counterculture Witness

The countercultural ideal is that there is always a society within the society and that the society within (in this case the church) leads the other into change and reform. This hope is described by Michael Harper in his account of the achievement of community in the Church of the Redeemer in Houston: "They shared the conviction that the world would sit up and take notice of the church when they saw Christians living out and demonstrating a style of Christian living which was both sacrificial and different in this increasingly affluent society of our day."[48]

This is also the conviction of the more radically oriented communities that back off from nearly all involvements in society. For example, Benjamin Zablocki, in describing the Bruderhof community, writes that "it is essential to the ideology of bearing witness that the achievements of the Bruderhof in creating an intentional community be perceived by the world as the achievements of exceptional men. The witness to community is a witness that this way of life is possible for all men."[49]

What is important, of course, is not just that the community exists but that its interior life is characterized by *the sharing of resources, a family spirit, simplicity, and healing.*

The Sharing of Resources

The ideal of sharing resources to which all Christian communities point is the experience of the earliest church recorded in Acts 2:43-46. Michael Harper points out that it was "an act of human compassion to meet human needs, not a sentimental form of idealism." Moreover, it was done in the context of worship, witness, and service, and no doubt was a major contribution to the flexibility and effectiveness of the early church's resources particularly in terms of manpower and deployment."[50]

Although a minority of Christians in the history of the church have lived in a sharing community, there has always been a community witness in the world, especially through the monastic orders. But the radical Christian argues that living in a community of shared resources is not a "vocation" for the few but rather the standard calling for all disciples of Jesus Christ.

To begin with, Jesus Christ Himself gave up all that He had to become human, to die for man, and to give him new life. Therefore His disciples are not to cling to anything; they are to be willing to set aside all that they have for others. Furthermore, radical Christians are fond of pointing out that everything belongs to Christ by virtue of creation and redemption. Therefore, no Christian ought to use what he possesses without keeping in mind the needs of his brothers and sisters. Sharing is rooted in an unselfish love. Christians belong to a brotherhood, and to act according to motives other than that of love is to act selfishly and without reference to Christ, to whom ultimate allegiance is confessed. Furthermore, there is an eschatological dimension to sharing. The point is that the Christian community will ultimately share all things, both material and immaterial, in the kingdom. All present sharing points to the ultimate and complete sharing that belongs to the Christian community.

The extent to which goods are shared in this life, however, may vary from community to community. The spectrum extends from total collectivism to personal ownership of property accompanied by a spirit of openness and generosity toward the needs of others.

A Family Spirit

The Christian community is much more than a mere collection of people—it is the family of God. Members of Christ are brothers and sisters in the "household of faith."

For this reason many Christian communities are involved in what has become known as the "extended family." An extended family reaches beyond the borders of the nuclear family—that is, parents and their children—to include others within the life of the family. A home may consist of one or more nuclear families plus single, widowed, and divorced people, elderly people, and orphans. Together these people constitute a family that is modeled on mutual support and interdependence. Radical Christians would agree with Graham Pulkingham:

> I don't think that the Lord ever intended for complete self-sufficient community to exist just between two people. I don't mean by this that two people can't establish a very wholesome community, they can; but it seems that the purpose of this kind of relationship is to include others. The fact that in our society marriage has been turned in on itself is causing problems so deep that many couples don't want to face them.[51]

Simplicity

Another feature of radical obedience to Christ is simplicity, in both personal and community life. At bottom, comments Vernard Eller, "the Christian simple life always is a positive doctrine of the enjoyment of God before it is a negative doctrine concerning the evil of the world."[52] It starts with the conviction that Christians are to "seek first the kingdom of God and then everything else will be added."

The simple life is one that is uncluttered by abundant possessions, the belief being that owning a lot of things leads to a preoccupation with preserving and protecting them. The positive aspect of simplicity is that it frees a person to develop the things that are really important in life—relationships, appreciation of beauty, the inner qualities of personhood. In the community where resources are shared and true simplicity is present, growth into union with Christ becomes a reality in every aspect of life.

Healing

Another characteristic of the inner life of the community is that it is a place where healing takes place. Chris Ellerman discusses this in *The Healing Process in Intentional Christian Communities.*[53] He defines healing as "a continual process of lifelong growth toward becoming everything mankind can be."[54] More specifically, this is expressed within the nurturing context of the community through the love and support provided—especially toward those who are struggling with their growth as a result of physical, mental, psychological, or spiritual handicaps.

CONCLUSION

We have looked at three historical examples of the separational model drawn from the ·pre-Constantinian church, the era of the Reformation, and the contemporary Western world. Although these groups vary considerably, they have some significant characteristics in common:

1. The central and most basic concern for the Christian is the way he lives his life. This does not mean that the separatists reject theology but that they see theology and theological disputes as secondary to the call to discipleship.

2. The Christian must live his life quite apart from the life of the world. This does not mean that the separatists reject the idea that a Christian lives in two worlds simultaneously, but that they believe he must make a conscious choice to live in the one and not the other as far as possible.

3. This life apart from the world is most effectively lived in communities. Communities take different shapes, ranging from radical communalism to task-achieving communities within the structure of the church that do not engage in household or economic sharing.

4. *The Christian community is the presence of the kingdom of God on earth.* The community is seldom equated with the kingdom. Instead, it is seen in an eschatological way as that which now shares in the kingdom and points to the ultimate kingdom of Christ.

5. *The interior life of the Christian community is controlled by the power of the Holy Spirit.* That is, the people of God evidence within themselves the fruits and gifts of the Holy Spirit, and this in itself sets them apart from the world.

Questions for Discussion

1. Scan this chapter and write down all those words and terms that are unfamiliar to you. Define them in your own words. What do these ideas have to do with the Christian in culture?
2. To what extent may the separatist approach to culture be determined by the cultural situation? Does the American cultural situation demand a separatist stance today?
3. Should today's church be a countercultural movement? What are the advantages and disadvantages of this approach to culture?
4. Make a list of ten ways you could live more simply.

Further Reading

Bloesch, Donald G. *Wellsprings of Renewal: Promise in Christian Communal Life.* Grand Rapids: Eerdmans, 1974.
Delespesse, Max. *The Church Community: Leaven and Life-Style.* Notre Dame: Ave Maria, 1973.
Eller, Vernard. *The Simple Life.* Grand Rapids: Eerdmans, 1973.
Estep, William R. *The Anabaptist Story.* Grand Rapids: Eerdmans, 1975.
Friedman, Robert. *The Theology of Anabaptism.* Scottdale, Pa.: Herald, 1973.
Grant, Robert M. *Early Christianity and Society.* New York: Harper, 1977.
––––––. *The Sword and the Cross.* New York: Macmillan, 1955.
Hershberger, Guy F. *The Recovery of the Anabaptist Vision.* Scottdale, Pa.: Herald, 1957.
Jackson, David and Neta. *Living Together in a World Falling Apart.* Carol Stream, Ill.: Creation House, 1974.
Sider, Ron. *Rich Christians in an Age of Hunger.* Downers Grove, Ill.: InterVarsity, 1977.
Williams, George H. *The Radical Reformation.* Philadelphia: Westminster, 1962.
Yoder, John H. *The Politics of Jesus.* Grand Rapids: Eerdmans, 1972.
Zablocki, Benjamin. *The Joyful Community.* Baltimore: Penguin, 1971.

6

The Identificational
Model

We have seen that the central point about the Christian's life in the world is that he must live under two rules simultaneously. The problem for each person and for the church is finding out how to do this.

The separatist's answer is to live in one world and not the other; he draws a sharp distinction between the two. The identifier, on the other hand, feels uncomfortable with this antitheis and seeks to resolve the problem through *paradox*. The paradoxical approach sees both sides of an issue and resolves it by affirming that both sides are true. The Christian is to live both in the kingdom of Christ and in the world. Exactly how this is accomplished is not necessarily agreed upon by all those who agree that the Christian life in the world is a paradox. Consequently, a variety of approaches fall under the general heading of "identificational." We will discuss three in particular, drawing from the Constantinian church, the Lutheran ideal, and the problem of civil religion. But first a word about the biblical basis for the identificational model.

THE BIBLICAL BASIS

The identifier insists that the Bible abounds in examples of believers who played a leading role in culture. For example, Joseph rose to the position of second in command to Pharaoh in Egypt. He was set "over all the land of Egypt" and was arrayed in garments of fine linen. A gold chain was put around his neck and as he rode in the chariot, people called out, "Bow the knee!" (Gen. 41:41-43). Likewise, Daniel was given a position of authority in Babylon. He was one of three presidents over the 120 satraps under whom the entire government was organized. Daniel became the most distinguished of these presidents, so that "the king planned to set him over the whole kingdom" (Dan. 6:1-3).

Jesus Himself was identified with the world: the Son of man "came eating and drinking, and they say, 'Behold, a glutton and a drunkard, a friend of tax collectors and sinners!'" (Matt. 11:19). Jesus also had friends in government, such as Nicodemus, and insisted as well that His followers "render . . . to Caesar the things that are Caesar's" (Matt. 22:21).

Furthermore, the accounts of the early church in Acts indicate that Christians were drawn from all areas of life and that no demand was made that they turn away from their occupations. This is true with the Ethiopian eunuch in Acts 8; Cornelius the centurion in Acts 10; Manaen, a member of the court of Herod the tetrarch, in Acts 13; and the Philippian jailor in Acts 16. The same kind of evidence is found in the Epistles. In Paul's letter to the Philippians written from jail in Rome he said, "All the saints greet you, especially those of Caesar's household" (4:22).

Even more important is the direct teaching of the Epistles concerning the Christian's duty toward the government. Paul in Romans 13 clearly sets forth the rule of government as an arena in which God is at work. In admonishing Christians to be subject to the governing authorities, Paul insists that "there is no authority except from God, and those that exist have been instituted by God" (v. 1). He calls the rulers of the world "ministers of God" and insists that we are to treat them as such, thus suggesting that work in the government is a high and perhaps even holy calling.

These biblical examples are furthermore substantiated by the theological undergirding of the doctrines of Creation, Incarnation, and redemption and by the understanding that the Christian is *simul justus et peccator*, both just and a sinner at the same time. The doctrine of Creation teaches that this is God's good world, that all of it belongs to Him. The doctrine of the Incarnation teaches that Christ assumed the created order and participated in it. The doctrine of redemption insists that because God is the creator and because the creator assumed the creation, the whole creation, through the life and death of Jesus Christ, has been redeemed (potentially). Therefore the Christian is *simul justus et peccator*. Before God he is saved, but in the world he is still a sinner. This same paradoxical principle is true of creation. Because of Christ, the creation has been released from its bondage to decay. But it will still be under decay and in bondage until the Second Coming, when God's redemptive work will be consummated. Consequently, the justified sinner and also the created order are caught in the tension between what is and what will be. In the context of this tension "all things are lawful." The Christian is free to affirm all of creation, to enter all callings, and to work and live before God in every aspect of life.

These principles were first expressed broadly in the church in the Constantinian era.

THE CONSTANTINIAN CHURCH

We have seen that the church during the first three centuries after Christ emphasized its opposition to the world. At the same time the state opposed the church and sought in various ways to suppress it. The most severe attempt to destroy the church was made in 303 under Diocletian. Three edicts, resulting from a devotion to paganism, were issued against the Christians in the hopes that their growth and influence would be destroyed.

A complete reversal was taken by Constantine, who, after his conversion to Christianity, issued the Decree of Toleration in 311 and the Edict of Milan in 313. The significance of these edicts for the relation between church and state is put this way by Charles Norris Cochrane: "By admitting the victory of Christianity over the secular order, it brought to a sudden and unexpected end the phase of opposition between the two; and by demonstrating, as nothing else could have done, the utter bankruptcy of the ancient religio-political idea, it pointed the way to a development of fresh relationships between the empire and the church."[1]

The Edict of Milan introduced four favorable new provisions for the Christian. First, it guaranteed Christians the right to profess the faith; second, it guaranteed them the right to gather for worship without fear of reprisal; third, it called for the restitution of buildings and land that had been confiscated from the church; and fourth, it recognized the corporate nature of the church by allowing it to hold property.[2]

This change in the state's attitude toward the church resulted in the principle of toleration toward all religions (changed by Theodosius in 378 when, by decree, Christianity became the only religion tolerated in the empire). This neutrality toward all religions actually made it possible for Christians to think in terms of a Christian social philosophy. It was out of this context, then, that a new idea was born: a Christian commonwealth. In the commonwealth, church and state would be no longer antithetical but complementary. This idea and the reality of it was not born or realized overnight. But it already began to be foreshadowed in the favorable disposition of the state toward the church.

The State Favors the Church

Even though the Edict of Milan promulgated a divorce between church and state, Constantine's personal religion was rapidly becoming the religion of the state. Before long it was evident that Constantine sought to help the church in two ways. First, he issued a series of decrees that led to the full legal equality of Christianity and, second, he supported the church politically.

His concern to give the church full equality was first expressed in his decree to Anulinus, proconsul of Africa in 313. In this decree he ordered the restoration of all church property. "Make haste," he wrote "to have restored to them with all speed all things before belonging to them by right, whether gardens or buildings or whatever they may be."[3] In another decree written in the same year to Calcilian, bishop of Carthage, he arranged for the payment of a sum of money to the church and indicated that, should it not be enough, more was available.[4] Another unprecedented move occurred the next year, when bishops met at a synod at Arles. Many of these bishops who had suffered in the persecutions only a few years before were escorted to the synod by the chariot teams of Constantine. This was a privilege that, prior to this time, was granted only to imperial messengers and high government officials. Furthermore, Constantine issued certain edicts that gave the clergy authority in public matters. One edict gave the bishops equal authority with the magistrates. Another put the manumission—that is, the freeing—of slaves by the church on an equal basis with manumission by the magistrate.

Constantine also favored the church politically. In 321 he declared that Sunday was an official day of rest. The only exception to this was to be made for the farmer who needed to look after his crops. Furthermore, Constantine brought numerous Christians into positions of authority in government. Previously Christians had refused to participate in the government because to do so would have involved them in pagan festivals and sacrifice. But now all this had changed, and the government was filled with Christians on every level. Constantine was busily shaping the Roman Empire into a Christian world empire. He paid particular attention to the city of Rome and attempted to make it the Christian capital of the world by putting Christians in responsible positions and by providing money for the construction of churches.[5]

All this, of course, had an effect on the church and on its attitude toward the state.

The Church Favors the State

The church, which only a few years before had faced the possibility of extinction by persecution, now, because of the conversion of Constantine, faced the possibility of creating a Christian empire. The unexpected triumph of the church was viewed as evidence of the hand of God. And it shifted attention away from a preoccupation with the future kingdom in heaven to the possible expression of that kingdom on earth. The promise of the dominion of Christ over the world was at hand.

The great church historian Eusebius, who was a personal friend of Constantine and his right-hand man during the Nicene Council, expressed the vision of a Christian society. In his *Oration* he speaks of the changes in the Roman Empire as a result of Constantine's conversion.

> Discourses and precepts, and exhortations to a virtuous and holy life, are proclaimed in the ears of all nations. Nay, the emperor himself proclaims them: and it is indeed a marvel that this mighty prince, raising his voice in the hearing of all the world, like an interpreter of the almighty Sovereign's will, invites his subjects in every country to the knowledge of the true God.[6]

Even more than Eusebius, the philosopher-theologian Lactantius provides a clue to the spirit of the Constantinian age. In his celebrated *Divine Institutes* he looked back to a bygone era of peace, prosperity, and brotherhood that was lost when the worship of the true God was taken away. After that men "began to contend with one another, and to plot, and to acquire for themselves glory from the shedding of human blood."[7] Lactantius cites lust as the source of all the evils of society, such as the motivation of private gain, slavery, the selfish acquisition of goods, unjust laws, tyranny, and violence. But in due time, he contends, "God, as a most indulgent parent, when the last time approached, sent a messenger to bring back that old age, and justice which had been put to flight, that the human race might not be agitated by very great and perpetual errors."[8]

What Lactantius appears to envision is not so much a world that has been transformed by the gospel as a society that identifies itself with moral, social, and political goodness. His religion is an innocuous Christianity that calls on people to suppress their evil desires and to return to the goodness of the original man. It is more a curious blend of pagan humanitarianism and Christian appearance than a thoroughgoing application of kingdom preaching to the ills of society. As Cochrane states, "It clearly forecasts that era of 'godly and righteous' legislation, of generous but not excessive reform, which was to be the net contribution of Constantinianism to the Kingdom of God."[9]

The point is that under Constantine the church was unable to effect a real transformation of society. What did occur was little more than the amelioration of certain societal ills along with the projection of a society that would, at least in external form, look more and more like the kingdom Jesus proclaimed. What this meant for the church in the world we will look at next.

The Church During the Constantinian Era

The significance of the shift that occurred in the church between the third and fourth centuries cannot be overemphasized. From the church against the state to the church for the state—that is indeed a long distance. It represents two completely different conceptions of the Christian and the church in the world. Not surprisingly, this situation had both negative and positive effects on the church.

In the first place, the church became a wealthy institution. In the past the clergy had been involved in small business enterprises as a means of supporting the church, and, of course, the church was quite dependent on donations by its members. But now, as the huge expansion of the church throughout the empire required the building of numerous new churches, the acquisition of art, and an increasingly elaborate system of administration, the church began to invest heavily in order to meet its expenses. The temptation of wealth and business was at least great enough that the Nicene Council produced a canon saying that any ecclesiastic found guilty of usury would be unfrocked.

A second problem for the church was that it became filled with nominal Christians. In the days of persecution to be a Christian was not only unpopular but a threat to one's life. There was no "cheap grace" in the early church; it cost a person something to be a follower of Christ. For this reason the doors of the church were open only to the faithful. Involvement in the church came only after an intense three-year period of catechetical teaching followed by baptism. But now the doors of the church were flung open. It was "popular" to be a Christian; the requirements, at least superficially, appeared to some to be little more than that the convert acquire certain virtues and niceties that were expected of those who were "well-bred."

A third problem was that the sharp distinction between the ideal of the kingdom and the ideal of humanitarianism was lost. The danger, as we have seen with Lactantius, is that of confusing Christian moral teaching with similar ideas from the pagan philosophers. This confusion of Christian and pagan ideals served to blunt the edge of Christian eschatology. The hope was no longer in the kingdom to come, or in a thorough understanding of the presence of the kingdom in the world. Rather, the hope was in making the world a better place to live and in making it safe for Christianity.

Finally, the church became a powerful institution. Its members (many of them nominal) filled government and administrative posts throughout the empire, and the emperor continually favored the church. In time, the emperor, with the sanction of the church, turned against the pagan and Jewish elements of society and persecuted them. The hunted became the hunters. By 381 Theodosius I took measures against non-Christians and declared in the decree *Nulles habreticus* that "we permit no heretics to hold their unlawful assemblies in the towns. If they attempt any disturbance, we decree that their fury shall be suppressed and that they shall be expelled outside the walls of the cities."[10]

Nevertheless, true Christianity did not die out, and the majority of church leaders and fathers did not support the accommodation of Christianity to the mere "niceties" set forth by Lactantius. In fact, the state's support of the church created a situation in which certain positive features of the Christian faith were able to take hold.

In the first place, the relative peace allowed the Christian church to hammer out what has come to be the basic and foundational theology of the church. Both the Nicene Creed, which defines the Christian faith as trinitarian, and the Chalcedonian definition, which affirms the full humanity and divinity of Christ, were formulated. Also, the growing worldliness of the church gave rise to the monastic movements, which, after the fall of Rome, became the major carriers of the Christian faith into the medieval period.

The Constantinian church, then, is an expression of the identificational model. The church tended to identify with the goals of a humanitarian society, and popular Christianity as a result became somewhat nominal.

THE LUTHERANS

Luther's view of the Christian in culture is rooted in a basic dualism that he found at the very heart of the Christian understanding of life. Gerhard Ebeling observes:

> Luther's thought always contains an antithesis, tension between strongly opposed but related polarities: theology and philosophy, the letter and the spirit, the law and the gospel, the double use of the law, person and works, faith and love, the Kingdom of Christ and the Kingdom of the world, man as a Christian and man in the world, freedom and bondage, God hidden and God revealed.[11]

Luther's approach to the question of the Christian in culture builds on this dualism: there are two realms of existence, one for the non-Christian and the other for the Christian, although the Christian lives in both simultaneously.

According to Luther, the teaching that human existence is to be understood in two realms is rooted in Scripture. Certain passages dealing with the authority of the state (such as Romans 13 and 1 Peter 2:13-14, and Old Testament statements like Genesis 9:6 and Exodus 21:14,22 ff. that sanction the use of the sword) are for everybody. All God's creatures are under the authority of the state and are to abide by the divine laws of creation. But other passages, such as the Sermon on the Mount and the apostles' statement about the "law of Christ," refer only to Christians, who are to live not by love and not by force.[12] These biblical references point to the two realms of human existence: the first, rooted in Creation and the Fall, in which all people participate equally; the second, rooted in Jesus Christ and the church, in which only believers participate. This insistence that there is a Christian existence in Christ and a Christian existence in the world is the key to Luther's understanding of the relation between Christianity and culture.

While on the surface Luther's explanation of the two kingdoms appears complicated, it is basically simple. The diagram may help to focus on its simplicity. The larger circle represents the kingdom of this world, which rightfully belongs to God by creation. All human beings live in this world. The smaller circle represents the kingdom of Christ, which is made up of true believers only. Because the true believers are part of this world and because they belong to Christ, they wholly belong to two worlds. Satan does not have a kingdom as such. He does not own creation; it is God's. Instead, Sa-

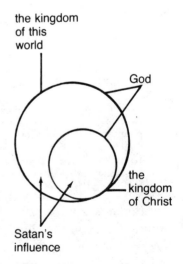

the kingdom of this world

God

the kingdom of Christ

Satan's influence

tan's influence extends throughout God's creation, beginning in the hearts of fallen men and extending through their exercise of authority over creation.

The Christian must, therefore, learn how to live his life before God in two existences at once. He is a saint because of his heavenly standing, and he is a sinner/saint because of his earthly existence. Exactly how the Christian is a citizen of two worlds simultaneously, and what this means to his way of life on earth, is a problem Luther continued to wrestle with throughout his life.[13]

In order to understand Luther's position more thoroughly, let us look first at the nature of the two realms, then at the rule of God in these realms, and finally at the application of all this to the life of the Christian in the world.

The Two Realms of Human Existence

In a treatise entitled "Temporal Authority" Luther speaks of the two realms of existence as two kingdoms:[14] "We must divide the children of Adam and all mankind in two classes, the first belonging to the Kingdom of God, the second to the Kingdom of the world. Those who belong to the Kingdom of God are all the true believers."[15]

The kingdom of this world originated in God's act of creation.[16] God not only brought the natural order into existence but also established the institutions of the world such as marriage and the family, business, and secular government. Consequently, everything earthly, temporal, and physical belongs to God, not to the devil, and is under His sovereign control. And so every human being, Christian or not, lives his life in this world under God. Man's rule over the earth is under God for the purpose of preserving earthly life.

On the other hand, the origin of the kingdom of God is rooted in redemption. God established a heavenly people for Himself through His act of redemption in Jesus Christ. Redeemed people belong to a spiritual kingdom that is at once in heaven and on earth.

God is at work in both realms of existence. His goodness,

love, and mercy are present through Jesus Christ, the Word, and the sacraments in the kingdom of God and through natural law, providence, and divine law in the kingdom of the world.

But there are differences between the two kingdoms and in the way God works in them. First, the kingdom of God outranks the kingdom of the world, because secular government serves only the world, which passes away, but the spiritual government of God serves eternal life and God's ultimate purpose. Second, there is an equality in the kingdom of God that does not exist in the kingdom of the world: in the priesthood of believers, all Christians stand on an equal plane before God; but in the kingdom of this world there are differences between people in the variety of functions necessary to govern the world. Some have positions of authority and others of dependence. Third, God rules by love, justice, forgiveness, and the Holy Spirit in the kingdom of God but by justice, retribution, punishment, and reason in the kingdom of the world.

Nevertheless, the two kingdoms are dependent on each other. The kingdom of this world creates the atmosphere of peace in which the kingdom of Christ is able to carry out its function. The gospel could never create peace because it doesn't force people to do anything. On the other hand, the preaching of the gospel results in good works, and this helps to stabilize society and reduce evil in the world.

In the kingdom of God the Christian is a saint, but in the kingdom of the world he is a sinner/saint.[17] Herein lies a further dualism that complicates our understanding of Luther. In the world the believer is both sinner and saint at the same time—not partially the one and partially the other, but wholly both. That is, before God he is a saint, but before man he is a sinner/saint, working out in time, space, and history the reality of his membership in the invisible community of believers. This is Luther's doctrine of gradual sanctification, a doctrine that accounts for the believer's lack of perfection in his existence in the world.

This dualism that characterizes the believer's personal life is also expressed on a more corporate level in his function in church and society. In the church the believer functions under the rule of Christ, both immediately, in personal submission to Christ, and mediately, in submission to God's appointed ministers of His Word. In society the believer functions under the rule of God immediately by obeying the laws of creation and mediately by living in submission to God's appointed rulers in the land. The unbeliever may also function in the church without being a part of God's invisible kingdom. The wheat and the tares grow together also in the church, a fact that points once again to Luther's basic theme of the dualism that permeates every aspect of human existence.

God's Rule in Each Realm

Implicit in Luther's presentation of the two kingdoms is the notion that God's government over this world can be understood only through a double expression. His rule is one thing in the kingdom of the world and another in the kingdom of God. Yet there are not two distinct rules, as though the unbeliever were under one set of laws and the believer another. Instead, both rules affect everyone in two different areas of the same life.

This approach is consistent with the dualistic motif of Luther's thought. But Luther would not want us to divide life into two distinct parts, the secular and the sacred. Instead, he is asking us to stand in God's place, as it were, and see our world and ourselves as He sees it. When God sees His creation, He sees it divided between the believer and the unbeliever, the church and society. But He sees His rule in the believer having an effect on the unbeliever, who cannot escape the presence of the kingdom of God in its earthly manifestation. And since God also rules in the kingdom of the world, His rule affects everyone in both his earthly and his spiritual existence. God rules over the whole person. These thoughts are most clearly presented in "Temporal Authority," where Luther wrote:

> God has ordained two governments: the spiritual, by which the Holy Spirit produces Christians and righteous people under Christ; and the temporal, which restrains the un-Christian and wicked so that—no thanks to them—they are obliged to keep still and to maintain an outward peace.[18]

A closer examination of God's rule in each of these two kingdoms will help to clarify this distinction. We will look first at the rule of God in the kingdom of the world.

Luther frequently refers to the two uses of the law, the spiritual and the civil.[19] The spiritual use of the law is to show man his sin and drive him to Christ. The civil use of the law is to function as a restraining and ordering influence in society.

Civil law, which is the law by which God governs the kingdom of the world, is, no less than spiritual law, in the world by "God's will and ordinance." It is divinely instituted and as old as creation itself. This rule, which Luther sometimes calls the "law of the temporal sword," is set forth in Romans 13 and 1 Peter 2:13-14. It also finds expression throughout the Old Testament, beginning with God's dealing with Cain. It was confirmed after the Flood, again in the law of Moses, and finally in the teaching of Jesus (Matt. 26:52).

This rule of God in the temporal affairs of man is always expressed through the secular government, whose God-given responsibility is to rule in society. Here Luther's view of sin comes into view. Because man is "altogether sinful and wicked," God puts him under the law to restrain his wicked deeds. The law holds back the sinfulness of man. It keeps the world from destroying itself through its own wickedness.

The law has a positive use also: it promotes goodness. Through political authorities and the laws of the land, people are protected from evil men. For this reason Luther can refer to the authorities as "saviors" and give them the same recognition attributed to fathers and mothers and doctors and lawyers whose help men cannot do without.

Justice, therefore, serves both a negative and a positive function: it punishes the wrongdoer and it encourages peace. For this reason the government is to be obeyed and honored by all people.

The second area of the rule of God is in the kingdom of God. In the spiritual kingdom all true believers are under Christ, who is King in God's kingdom. Christ came into the world to establish God's kingdom in the world, a kingdom that is not "of the world." In this kingdom there is no need of the temporal law or the sword, for Christians are ruled by the Holy Spirit, who teaches them "to do injustice to no one, to love everyone, and to suffer injustice and even death willingly and cheerfully at the hands of anyone."[20]

How are these two rules of God related? Because man's temporal existence and spiritual existence are both under God, Luther argues that "neither one is sufficient in the world without the other." We must recognize the need for both, "the one to produce righteousness, the other to bring about external peace and prevent evil deeds."[21]

However, the one must not invade the territory of the other and presume to rule where it has no right. The temporal government, for example, has laws that extend no further than to matters of life and property and external affairs on earth, for God will not permit anyone but Himself to rule over the soul. For the state to attempt in any way to coerce people into belief would be a violation of its function, an invasion of a realm not under its jurisdiction. Only God Himself, through the Spirit, creates belief; the heart cannot be compelled against its will.

On the other hand, the rule and authority of the priests and bishops has—contrary to the example of the medieval period—nothing to do with man's temporal existence. Their government, Luther insists (on the basis of the priesthood of all believers), is "not a matter of authority or power, but a service." In their Christian existence believers are ruled only by God's Word, which instructs them in all matters pertaining to their spiritual existence.

The Christian lives under both rules. While Luther separates the two and speaks of man's existence under God's secular authority and the Christian man's existence under Christ or biblical authority, he does not mean to separate them as though the believer lived *only* under the authority of Christ,

nor does he bring the two together in such a way to make the
believer appear schizophrenic. He is viewing two aspects of
the same existence.

The Christian man lives under the Word of God in his
spiritual existence and the secular authority in his temporal
existence. He owes obedience to both under God. For this
reason, says Luther, the Christian "submits most willingly to
the rule of the sword, pays his taxes, honors those in authority,
serves, helps, and does all he can to assist the governing authority, that it may continue to function and be held in honor
and fear."[22]

Not only does the Christian submit to the law of the
sword, but he is also encouraged by Luther to "serve and
assist the sword" because it is "beneficial and essential for the
whole world and for your neighbor." However, while Luther
encourages the believer to participate in every aspect of society, he insists that the Christian should never use secular
authority for himself or his cause. Rather, he "should wield it
[the sword] and invoke it to restrain wickedness and to defend
godliness" on behalf of his neighbor. The Christian can serve
in this area because it is a "divine service."

Here again we are confronted by the tension that the
Christian finds himself in. He is to serve the secular authority
in temporal matters, living according to a law that appears
contradictory to his Christian persuasion. This is the problem
of Christian existence in the world.

The Christian in the World

Luther's position on the Christian in the world cannot be
understood apart from his interpretation of the Sermon on the
Mount.[23] In interpreting the Sermon, Luther had to oppose
two strongly and widely held convictions that Jesus' teachings
in this passage could be practiced only by those who completely withdrew from the world. For one, the official Roman
Catholic position was that the ethical teachings contained in
the Sermon were intended not as unconditional *commandments*

for everyone but only as *counsels* for those who wished to achieve perfection. This position fit the Roman Catholic view that there are two stages of discipleship for Christians. In the second stage, the ascetic ideal, one attempts to fulfill the requirements of Jesus in the strictest sense by withdrawing from the world into a monastic community

On the other hand, Luther had to define himself over against the Anabaptists, who also insisted on a radical obedience achievable only through a complete forsaking of the world and its ways. It meant a refusal to participate in the institutions of the world, in its occupations, and in its power. True discipleship could be expressed only in Christian communities cut off from the outside world, where Christians were free to create a whole new way of life, a culture, in conformity with the teachings of Christ. While the majority of Anabaptists withdrew to form their own culture, a small minority of Anabaptist millenarians were convinced that it was their responsibility to revolutionize the world, reshaping it to live by the standards of the kingdom, and thus bringing about the kingdom of God on earth. These active enthusiasts are the ones Luther came up against in the Peasants' War.

Luther's interpretation of the Sermon on the Mount is consistent with the dualism that runs through his entire approach to the Christian faith. His perception is rooted in his view of freedom and love. The freedom to which Christ calls us must govern our attitude toward the material goods of the world. Luther warns us against making material goods too important, thus raising them to the status of idols in our lives. Freedom is therefore an inner quality, an attitude of the heart toward possession. Owning property and enjoying this earth's goods are not inherently wrong. This is God's world, and His ownership extends over all things. But we are to be free from the service of this world's goods. We are not to set "our confidence, comfort, and trust on temporal goods." Poverty is therefore an inner thing, a matter of the heart. We are not to be attached to earthly goods in any way. This is the inner freedom that Paul describes in 2 Corinthians 6:10, as "having nothing, and yet possessing everything," Sometimes God may call a person to abandon earthly possessions, literally, but this would be the exception. Nevertheless, the believer must be ready at all times to drop everything if God should so demand. For Luther, this position is never an excuse to accumulate riches. He himself lived a frugal life. He insisted that the believer should not own more than he really needed, giving the rest to his neighbors and to the poor.

Although Christians live by freedom in the realm of material goods, they live by love in human relationships. For Luther, the standard of love extends not only toward other believers in the kingdom of God but also toward the unbelievers in the kingdom of this world. Although man is free economically to own property and to trade and free politically to support the state or serve as a judge or statesman or soldier, he must always do so by the ethic of love. Love forgives, suffers injustice without demand for retribution, and places the interest of others above its own. Love creates a style of life in utter antithesis to the selfishness and greed of the normal sinful approach to life.

Through freedom and love, Luther believed, the Christian is able to live in the world in a manner consistent with the teaching of Jesus in the Sermon on the Mount. From this arose Luther's view of Christian calling.

Like everything else, Luther's view of calling is rooted in the dualistic understanding of Christian existence in two realms:[24] there is the invisible and spiritual calling where the believer is totally just in Christ; and there is a calling in life where the believer actively lives out his sanctification.

Luther's view of the sacredness of all callings in life was forged against the common notion that certain aspects of life were spiritual and others secular. Unlike the Roman Catholics, who confined spiritual callings to the priesthood, monastic life, or other service within the church, Luther insisted that all believers were equally justified before God and that therefore all functions of believers in the world were the areas in which they were called to live as believers, demonstrating their justification and working out their sanctification. The believer's life in this world is the place where he is called to live out, in freedom and love, his heavenly or spiritual standing. Consequently Luther can refer to every "estate" (a word he used to mean a person's specific function) as a calling in life that is ultimately spiritual in nature. A priestly estate is no more sacred than that of a teacher, carpenter, or prince.

However, this view of the equality of all callings did not keep Luther from making distinctions among the estates. This is clearly seen in his so-called three hierarchies: the priestly office, the married estate, and the world magistracy. These are special callings in which persons are more able to fight the devil. But they are no more spiritual than any other calling, and they are not means by which man is able to do good to obtain salvation.

For Luther, marriage belongs in the kingdom of this world.[25] Love, marriage, sexual desire, and parenthood are all a part of God's natural order, ordained in the creative act of God. God told man to "be fruitful and multiply," and He sanctified marriage and sexual love, not only for procreation but also for man's enjoyment and pleasure.

But because of sin, love is no longer pure. Persons seek to satisfy themselves rather than their partners. Consequently the physical joy of marriage has become lustful; conception has lost its purity, as the psalmist indicated: "Behold, I was brought forth in iniquity, and in sin did my mother conceive me" (Ps. 51:5). Because of sin, marriage has an added dimension: it restrains and controls sexuality, which, because it has been distorted by sin, now needs limits. Even in marriage the impurity of lustful desires cannot be avoided, so people in this order of creation, as in others, are not able to escape sinning. But God forgives married people of this sin because marriage is His work; He instituted it and continues to will it.

Because marriage is for everyone and belongs to the order of creation rather than the order of redemption, Luther does not view marriage as a sacrament and speaks of it as a secular affair. It is under the jurisdiction of the state, not the church;

subject to civil law, not ecclesiastical law.[26] This does not mean, though, that there is no difference between a Christian and a non-Christian marriage. Christians have the power of the Holy Spirit and the love of Christ (depicted as a marriage relationship between Himself and the church) to enable them to fulfill the ideal of marriage better than non-Christians do.

Work is also related to God's natural law and belongs to the kingdom of this world.[27] God ordained work before the Fall: Adam was given responsibility to till and to keep the garden of Eden. Therefore work is an honorable thing and a sphere in which we can expect to find God's blessing.

Because of sin, work is also a tiresome and burdensome responsibility. It involves toil, discouragement, and difficulty. Man must often fight against the elements to make his living by the "sweat of his brow." And people who see things through the eyes of the flesh see work mainly in this way. But for the Christian there is a difference, because he sees work through the eyes of the Holy Spirit. The believer knows that his work is a form of obedience to God and is therefore approved by Him. So, though man's labors are under a curse, they are also under a blessing; work is meaningful and ultimately of great personal value.

The ownership of property also belongs to the kingdom of this world.[28] Luther could not find any specific statements in the Bible affirming the right of private ownership. Therefore he comes at the question in a rather round-about way. He argues, for example, that Jesus' statement "sell what you have" presupposes private property, as does the biblical injunction to give to one's neighbor. If we do not have anything, we are not able to give. Therefore private ownership must be ordained of God.

Although Luther rejects the communism of radical Anabaptists, he does insist that the Christian is called upon to make his property available to those who are in need. Of course, he is to meet the needs of his own family first. But what is left over belongs to his neighbor. For the most part, Luther viewed business and the money economy of his time as corrupt. For Luther, business is motivated mostly by the selfish desire for profit. Consequently, he argued against usury and insisted that people look for a reasonable way to arrive at prices through an analysis of cost.

The state is also a part of the kingdom of this world.[29] The state is an order created by God, and like everything else He has created, it is good.

But the *function* of government in the world is shaped by the Fall. Because of sin, human beings have become wicked and perverse in their ways and need control lest they destroy themselves. The purpose of government in this fallen world, then, is to protect the people under its care against the cruelty and exploitation of their fellow men. It preserves peace and order. But it performs its duty as a parent, as one who cares for those whom it controls. In this sense the government stands before the people as God. It rewards the good and punishes the evil so that God's goodness and His wrath are known through the administration of government. Therefore the government has power over life and death, the power to impose the death penalty or to wage war.

Now the Christian, who lives both in the kingdom of God and in the kingdom of the world, is to act responsibly toward God in both realms. Because the state is God's work and because God rules through the state, the Christian's existence in the world is under God through the state. He is to be obedient to the state and to serve and assist the state. Even if the state acts unjustly, he is still to obey its dictates. Only if the state forces the Christian to act contrary to God's Word does its authority over the Christian end.[30]

Luther's view of the church in the world follows the same pattern as his view of the Christian in the world. The church is to be found in two realms of existence. In the heavenly realm it is totally just before God, but in its earthly and visible manifestation it expresses itself simultaneously in both the kingdom of God and the kingdom of the world. Consequently, its existence in Christ is as a spiritual and internal communion while its existence in the world is as an external communion.[31]

The problem here is to understand the relation of the outward, visible communion to both the kingdom of God and the kingdom of the world. Luther rejects outright the notion of a pure church without sin. For one thing, the church is "mixed," containing sinners who are not part of the internal communion. Furthermore, even the Christians in the church are sinners. So the church, at its best, is both just and sinful simultaneously.

Luther regarded the church, in its outward form, as a mask. The mask is its costume or shell in which it is heard, seen, and grasped. A mask may be the kind of building used, the time of service, the organization of the church, and even the authority of any person in the organization such as a pastor or a bishop. In these *masks,* God is hidden. But there are also *signs* through which God reveals Himself, and these are the preaching of the Word and the sacraments. Masks, therefore, belong to the kingdom of this world and signs to the kingdom of God. So the Christian in the church, as in other aspects of society, finds himself wholly in both realms of existence.

Conclusion

As we have seen, Luther's primary point of emphasis is the dualism between the two realms of human existence for the Christian. This concept of dualism is rooted in the beliefs that Creation is good, the Fall introduced an element of disorder into God's good order, and redemption in Christ is the only means for man's reconciliation. Luther's dualism makes a very positive contribution to a realistic assessment of the believer's role in society. Man is involved in the sins of the world. He cannot escape participation in the rebellion against God from which he has been redeemed. As Paul described it in Romans 7, the believer is tossed between what he is and what he ought to be. He can never fulfill his heavenly existence on earth, simply because he is in an earthly existence. He is still a creature of the world, a prisoner of his sinful nature.

But the believer is not thereby free to do whatever he

wants, to be licentious or reckless in his role in God's world. For, as we have seen, Luther stresses the need to be a responsible Christian, living in the world according to the transcendent principles of the Sermon on the Mount, which can indeed be lived out in the world and need not be relegated to some ascetic or other separate existence. In this way the Christian will function as a creative and dynamic force within society, bringing the gospel of the kingdom of God to bear on the structures of the kingdom of this world.

CIVIL RELIGION

Our third example of identificational Christianity, civil religion, does not recognize a tension between the church and the world. The church sees the role of the nation in the world as a role ordained by God. Therefore the church tends to support a "national calling" by seeing the spiritual and temporal goals of the church fulfilled through the national consciousness and activity—through social legislation, political influence, and economic stability as well as the expansion of the nation's influence around the world. In this way Christ shines through the culture. This view of the relation between Christ and culture may be designated "accommodation Christianity" or "culture Christianity."

Defining the Term

Historians and theologians find civil religion to be an element in the relation between the church and the world almost from the church's beginnings, but particularly after Constantine. However, an exact definition of civil religion has eluded the scholars. There is no general agreement on the meaning of the term.

Russell Richey and Donald Jones, in a collection of essays entitled *American Civil Religion*, have attempted to isolate "five meanings of civil religion."[32] Their analysis can help us get a grasp on the issue. They conclude that within American civil religion one can speak about folk religion, a transcendent universal religion of the nation, a religious nationalism, a democratic faith, and a Protestant civic piety. Of these five categories of civil religion, the first three may be found in practically every civilization. The last two are peculiar to the Anglo-Saxon experience.

Folk religion may be identified as those religious ideas, values, symbols, ceremonies, and loyalties that most of the people of any nation hold in common. These may include such things as belief in the existence of God and a positive attitude toward morality, the Bible, church attendance, and prayers at important public events. The *transcendent universal religion* of the nation is harder to grasp. In the nonpluralistic societies of medieval Europe or Russia before the revolution, the transcendent religion would be Catholicism or Orthodoxy. But in a modern pluralistic society, the transcendent religion is above identification with any particular form of faith. It points rather to such ideas of faith as God's purpose for the nation. *Religious nationalism* has to do with those aspects of religion that support patriotism as a religious virtue and glorify the nation by calling for dedication to it and personal sacrifice for its sake. The last two, *the democratic faith* and *Protestant civic piety,* are peculiarly Western and represent an intermingling of the norms and goals of the church with those of the state.

It was Jean-Jacques Rousseau (1712-78) who first used the term *civil religion.* He attempted to resolve the problem of the tension between religion and culture in a pluralistic society by speaking of a "social contract." He recognized that no state could exist without having some kind of religion at its base. But he chided Christianity because he felt that it weakened the state by setting forth a dual allegiance for believers. He sought to solve this problem through the creation of a civil religion, which he identified as "a purely civil profession of faith." This would provide the "social sentiments without which a man cannot be a good citizen or a faithful subject." He insisted that these sentiments should be "few, simple, and exactly worded" and suggested they include "the existence of a mighty, intelligent, and beneficent Divinity, possessed of foresight and providence, the life to come, the happiness of the just, the punishment of the wicked, the sanctity of the social contract and the laws."[33] In other words, he saw religion as the moral glue that held society together. It was the will of the people expressed religiously within the state. Consequently the state assumes a religious character.

Civil Religion in Western History

What Rousseau described was not at all his own invention. He merely gave a name to a phenomenon that had existed for centuries in the Western world.

It is generally accepted that the pagan states of Greece and Rome were modeled on a kind of civil religion. Because the Christian religion could not support Roman civil religion, it suffered persecution. The change that came with Constantine has been interpreted by some as a shift toward a Christian civil religion in the Roman Empire. However, it is usually held that a return to civil religion in terms of a universal, state-oriented faith did not occur until the twelfth and thirteenth centuries.

Although the medieval period may be seen as a contest between papal and monarchical power, it was in fact monarchical power that generally ruled the day. Power rested in a monarchical civil religion. The king was considered the direct agent of God. From Paul's teaching of the mystical body was derived a view that men were joined together morally and politically under their head the king in the same way that men were joined spiritually to Christ. All members of the body politic were to be directed by the head and to serve the head. The king's peace was the peace of the church. His battles became the battles of the church.

In the meantime the church developed a similar consciousness about itself. It saw itself as the supreme ruler over both the state and the church. The church declared itself to be *corpus mysticum*, the mystical body of Christ on earth. All things and all people, including kings, were to be under its jurisdiction, for through the church Christ ruled in the world.

When king and pope clashed over ultimate power, the

subjects were forced to choose the one to whom they would be loyal. With the emergence of nationalism and the corruption of the late medieval church, the people of France, Germany, and England chose king over pope. It was not a choice, however, between a secular state and a religious state. The state was already a religious entity and the king was God's instrument through which His will would be carried out across the land. In this way the state achieved a religious status, and people began to think of their citizenship in religious and moral terms. Gradually the state and the church became independent bodies. But the state continued to promulgate moral and ethical values that were shaped by its relationship to the church.[34]

The Reformation and the Renaissance of the sixteenth century mark the transitional period from the medieval world to the modern world. During this period the church and the state became two distinct entities and the idea of a pluralistic society was born. This revolutionary change introduced new complexities into the problem of civil religion. For example, both nationalism and secularism substituted earthly goals and ends for what was once a transcendent goal. In this way the soil was prepared for the religious character of secular ideologies such as communism.

More important for our purposes, however, is the way in which the religious notion of the state has been carried over into what we call American civil religion.

American Civil Religion

The roots of American civil religion go back to England and its self-concept as a "chosen nation." This idea was popularized by John Foxe in his widely read *Book of Martyrs*. Foxe set forth the story of the suffering Protestants in such a way as to make England appear to be especially called by God to retain and spread the truth. England was God's chosen nation, and through it the divine plan of God would be fulfilled.

The Puritans brought this idea of an elect nation with

them to America. The hope of a new people of God is clearly seen in the famous words of John Winthrop:

> Wee shall finde that the God of Israell is among us, when tenn of us shall be able to resist a thousand of our enemies, when hee shall make us a prayse and glory, that men shall say of suceeding plantacions; the Lord make it like that of New England: for wee must consider that wee shall be as a citty upon a Hill, the eies of all people are uppon us. . . .[35]

During the eighteenth-century Great Awakening, the idea that America was a chosen nation was further strengthened by the preaching and influence of Jonathan Edwards. He encouraged people to gather for praser fr the coming of God's kingdom. It was his conviction that the Millennium, the thousand-year reign of Christ on earth, might come to America. Other revivalists picked up this theme, and through them a sense of special destiny was instilled in the American soul.

This sense was heightened through the American Revolution. Politicians and preachers alike compared the American situtation to Israel and the Exodus. The British were the Egyptians in hot pursuit of America, the New Israel. But God was on the American side even as He was on Israel's—and He would see America through its Red Sea and then through the wilderness to the Promised Land.

In the nineteenth century most evangelical preachers and leaders thought the Millennium would come as a result of the Christianization of the world. The great revivalists, such as Lyman Beecher and Charles G. Finney, were convinced that God had chosen America to lead the way in the moral and political emancipation of the world. It was America's destiny to prepare the world for the coming of Christ.

Gradually Protestants began to see the nation as the means through which God was working in history. The concept of a chosen people became that of a chosen nation. Against this background, the role of Christians in the spread of American imperialism is understandable. Spreading Americanism was equal to spreading Christianity, for it was in the American character that one could most clearly see the

character of God. Consequently an American messianic consciousness emerged; it was believed that America was to be
the savior of the world.[36]

Although the wars and depressions of the twentieth century, as well as the rapid spread of secularism, have eroded the
American messianic consciousness, a number of people still
find biblical Christianity and the American destiny in agreement. Richard Pierard in *The Unequal Yoke*[37] describes the
current phenomenon and questions its validity. In particular
he argues that evangelical Christianity is yoked to an un-
healthful political conservatism.

Pierard cites, as one of the reasons for this unequal yoke,
"the capture of the evangelical churches by business interests." This occurred through the business connections of D. L.
Moody and Billy Sunday, who were supported by magnates
like John Wanamaker, Cyrus McCormick, Cornelius Vander-
bilt II, and J. P. Morgan. One result of this alignment was the
growth of "successful Christianity": if you give your life to
Jesus, He will bless you and make you rich, popular, and
powerful. Says Pierard, "The tendency to emphasize results
for results' sake, and to justify whatever tended to produce
them, subtly but definitely diluted the good news of the gospel.
In time new elements crept into the evangelistic message such
as the middle-class success myth, American Chauvinism,
opposition to actions of organized labor, and of course pro-
hibition."[38]

Evangelical Christianity became identified with the *status
quo* and with the preservation of the culture that big business
had created, one that political conservatism tended to perpetuate in America and around the world. Gradually an unfortunate marriage occurred between evangelical Christianity
and the political right. Although this attitude began to break
down in the seventies with the emergence of a more critical
viewpoint among younger leaders, there is still a perverse
atmosphere of Americanism in evangelicalism and in other
branches of Protestantism as well. But its emphasis is on
maintaining individualism, the free enterprise system, and

freedom of speech and religion as marks of Christian teaching rather than on the older notion that Christian America will be the vehicle through which the Millennium will arrive. The blend of Christianity with the state now has, as a primary function, the maintenance of these values (as well as other Christian values) against the inroads of socialism, communism, or any form of totalitarianism.[39]

CONCLUSION

We have looked at three historical examples of the identificational model: the Constantinian church, the Lutheran ideal, and civil religion. Although there is considerable variety among these groups, they share these basic views:

1. *God works in the world through both the state and the church.* Both are ordained of God. The government rules over the secular affairs of mankind while the church rules in the sphere of the spiritual. Since both are ultimately under God's providence, there are ways in which they may naturally coincide.

2. *The Christian must live within a dual commitment.* Since he is under God both in the state and in the church, he is constantly caught in the tension between these spheres in matters of his time, talents, and energy.

3. *The greatest difficulty is in determining how to achieve the balance between man's life in Christ and his life in the world.* Because the demands are sometimes contradictory (for example, the service of the nation at war as opposed to a strict adherence to the principles of the Sermon on the Mount), the Christian is forced toward a dichotomy: a public and private, external and internal, secular and sacred.

Questions for Discussion

1. Scan this chapter and write down all those words and terms that are unfamiliar to you. Define them in your own words. What do these ideas have to do with the Christian in culture?

2. Compare the identifier with the separationalist. Which are you?
3. What similarities do you find between church and state in the Constantinian Era and church and state in your location?
4. Do you think that Lutheran dualism is a viable option for the Christian in culture today? Why?
5. Does your church background and your view of culture in any way reflect a national messianic consciousness?
6. List ten ways you identify with culture. Are you justified in this identification?

Further Reading

Alfoldi, Andrew. *The Conversion of Constantine and Pagan Rome.* Translated by Harold Mattingly. Oxford: Clarendon, 1948.

Althaus, Paul. *The Ethics of Martin Luther.* Philadelphia: Fortress, 1972.

Cochrane, Charles Norris. *Christianity and Classical Culture.* New York: Oxford University, 1957.

Crany, Edward F. *An Essay on the Development of Luther's Thought on Justice, Law and Society.* Cambridge: Harvard University, 1959.

Doerries, Hermann. *Constantine and Religious Liberty.* Translated by Roland H. Bainton. New Haven: Yale University, 1970.

_____. *Constantine the Great.* New York: Harper, 1972.

Ebeling, Gerhard. *Luther: An Introduction to His Thought.* Translated by R. A. Wilson. Philadelphia: Fortress, 1970.

Elert, Werner. *The Structure of Lutheranism.* Translated by Walter A. Hansen. St. Louis: Concordia, 1962.

Luther's Works, Volumes 44, 45, 46, 47. Philadelphia: Fortress, 1955–.

Luther: Selected Political Writings. Edited by J. M. Porter. Philadelphia: Fortress, 1974.

Marty, Martin E. *The New Shape of American Religion.* New York: Harper, 1959.

_____. *The Pro & Con Book of Religious America.* Waco: Word, 1975.

Niebuhr, Richard. *The Kingdom of God in America.* Hamden, Conn.: Shoe String, 1956.

Pierard, Richard U. *The Unequal Yoke.* Philadelphia: Lippincott, 1970.

7

The Transformational
Model

We come now to the third historic model, the transformational. It presents a view of how to live under the two rules simultaneously in a way that differs significantly from both the separational and the identificational models.

The major difference is the belief that the structures of life can be converted and changed. The transformationalist's view is not that of withdrawal, emphasized by the separatist; nor is it that of accommodation, which the identificationalist often slips into. Instead, the transformationalist advocates an optimistic position toward culture as central to the Christian conviction about history and life.

This does not mean that all who believe in this model agree about how and when change will take place. There are decided differences of opinion about this. But the hope for a transformed society remains the same. We will look at three such models represented by Augustine, Calvin, and the contemporary liberation movement. But first a brief look at the biblical basis of the transformational model.

THE BIBLICAL BASIS

The biblical teaching on transformation is found not in examples as such but rather in the theological consciousness of the biblical writers themselves. Specifically, this viewpoint is expressed in the theological teaching about Creation, redemption, and eschatology. It is integral to the biblical theology of salvation that (1) the world, though created good, has fallen; (2) subsequent culture expresses the fallen nature of man and the created order; (3) Jesus' death and resurrection reverse the fallen condition of man and his creation; and (4) the Christian hope is for the ultimate release of man and the creation from the bondage of sin into a new and perfect creation. This teaching, which is central to biblical theology, is taught especially in the eschatological hope of Israel, the redemptive works of Christ, and the eschatology of the New Testament.

The eschatological hope of Israel is particularly apparent in the prophetic literature. The prophets look for a time when the earth will be transformed. In that day the Lord will "create new heavens and a new earth" (Isa. 65:17) and "the wolf and the lamb shall feed together, the lion shall eat straw like the ox; and dust shall be the serpent's food" (v. 25). And in that day "the mountains shall drip sweet wine, and the hills shall flow with milk, and all the stream beds of Judah shall flow with water; and a fountain shall come forth from the house of the LORD and water the valley of Shittim" (Joel 3:18). Passages like this, which can be multiplied from the writings of the prophets, continually bring together creation and salvation. That is, the future salvation of Israel is not merely spiritual but earthly. The whole creation has been changed. Culture will someday be what it could have been before the Fall.[1]

The redemptive work of Christ is central to this restoration of Creation. Paul sets forth this theme in his Epistles. In Romans 5:12-21 he compares the first Adam with the second, Jesus Christ. The first Adam did something *to* the human race: he brought sin, death, and condemnation. The results of his action are seen within the created order, which is marked through and through with signs of death. Thus culture is under the judgment of God (Rom. 1:18-32). But the second Adam reversed the human situation. He did something *for* man. He brought righteousness, life, and justification. The point is that what Christ did, He did in a cosmic sense. He called into being a "new creation" (2 Cor. 5:17). Consequently, the whole created order now anticipates its ultimate release and renewal. As Paul states, "The creation waits with eager longing for the revealing of the sons of God; for the creation was subjected to futility . . . the creation itself will be set free from its bondage to decay . . . the whole creation has been groaning in travail together until now" (Rom. 8:19-22). This future hope of creation is rooted in the redemption of Christ even as Creation and redemption were connected in the Old Testament prophetic consciousness.

But Creation and redemption are not complete without eschatology. The redemption of the creation in the ultimate and complete sense is in the future. The church *now* participates in the process toward the future. But the complete redemption of the creation has not yet been finalized. The eschatology of the New Testament recognizes this and looks beyond the present order to the completion of Christ's redemptive work. Peter speaks of such a day—"the day of God, because of which the heavens will be kindled and dissolved, and the elements will melt with fire! But according to his promise we wait for new heavens and a new earth in which righteousness dwells" (2 Peter 3:12-13). The interpretation of this passage points to a cultural change, a passing away of evil and the release of the created order from its bondage to decay. And like the apostle John, it looks for a "new heavens and a new earth" (Rev. 21 and 22), which may be an image of what this earth will look like after God's salvation has been accomplished within it.

Having surveyed the general biblical basis from which the transformationalist works, we turn to some examples of the transformational position in history.

AUGUSTINE AND "THE CITY OF GOD"

Augustine's view of the relation of the Christian to culture is most clearly expressed in his work *The City of God*. What prompted him to write this was the accusation by the pagans that Christianity was responsible for the fall of Rome.

In the first five "books" of this work, Augustine refutes the popular notion that human happiness is derived from the worship of pagan deities and that the neglect of this worship results in disaster. In the next five books he demolishes the arguments of those who insist that the worship of pagan deities is important for the life to come. Finally, beginning in Book XI, he proceeds to develop the concept of "the two cities that are confused together in this world, and distinct in the other."

The Two Cities

The two cities are the city of God and the city of man. The city of God is made up of all those who follow the true God, whether they be inside or outside the church. Likewise, the city of man is made up of all those who worship false gods, whether they be inside or outside the church. Augustine defines these cities around the idea of two kinds of love: "The earthly city was created by self-love reaching the point of contempt for God, the heavenly city by the love of God carried as far as contempt of self. In fact, the earthly city glories in itself, the heavenly city glories in the Lord."[2] The two cities cannot, therefore, be identified as strict visible entities. They have a spiritual existence and find their way into opposite attitudes that come into conflict through man and the shape he gives to culture.

One must understand the origins of these two cities if one is to understand their character. The city of God originates with the creation of light (i.e., with the angels), and the city of man begins with the sin of Satan. Sin is not something that is intrinsic to creation. Rather, sin is a defect of will. God's creation is therefore not evil; created beings become evil by choice. What is true in the realm of angels is also true in the realm of the created world and man. When God created the world He knew full well that the unity of society, though desirable, would not be accomplished. Man too, would eventually form two opposing societies.

These two societies, though already present within Adam himself, emerge specifically in Cain and Abel. "Cain founded a city, whereas Abel, as a pilgrim, did not found one," says Augustine. "For the city of the saints is up above, although it produces citizens here below, and in their persons the city is on pilgrimage until the time of its Kingdom comes."[3] For this reason the one city is rooted in "worldly possession" and the other in "heavenly hopes."

Next, Augustine traces the history of these two cities from Noah to Abraham and from Abraham to David. Abraham is promised that he will be the spiritual father of the city of God. This promise is continued in the descendants of Abraham to David. David ruled in the earthly Jerusalem. At this time the prophecies of Christ became more clear, especially in the psalms. These prophecies were finally realized in the death and resurrection of Christ and the beginning of the church. In the meantime, the course of the city of man continued to parallel that of the city of God, and the city of man came to fruition in the Roman Empire. Nevertheless there is a mixture of the elect and the reprobate in the church as well as in the empire. The confusion between the city of God and the city of man will continue until the judgment, when they will be severed forever and receive the reward of their works.

This brief sketch of *The City of God* provides a general background against which we will look more specifically at the relation between (1) the state and the city of man and (2) the church and the city of God.

The State and the City of Man

Augustine does not equate the state with the city of man. As John Figgis points out, "The primary distinction is always between 'two societies, the body of the *reprobate* and the *communis sanctorum;* not between church and state."[4] For Augustine the state is human society organized, and as such it contains members of both the city of God and the city of man. This persuasion provides a clue to Augustine's transformational position. If those who control the state have at the same time a final commitment to God, their influence will be felt in the social order.

Because of the interplay between the state and the city of man and the city of God, it is impossible to pin Augustine down to a specific and manageable political view. Nevertheless, certain emphases are quite clear in his writing.

First, we may say that Augustine is not against the state as such, nor is he against the involvement of Christians in the administration of the state. He often quotes with approval the apostolic teaching on submission to the powers that be. He insists that Christians are to give to Caesar what belongs to him, and he values highly family life and social relationships.

However, Augustine does condemn the lust for power. "Is it reasonable, is it sensible," he asks, "to boast of the extent and grandeur of empire, when you cannot show that men lived in happiness, as they passed their lives amid the horrors of war. . . ?"[5]

Justice, not power, is the essence of the state. "Remove justice," he insists, "and what are kingdoms but gangs of criminals on a large scale? What are criminal gangs but petty kingdoms? A gang is a group of men under the command of a leader, bound by a compact of association, in which the plunder is divided according to an agreed convention."[6] The point is that justice cannot be had where the true God is not worshiped. Therefore true justice exists only in the society of God, and the time when this will be truly fulfilled is only after the judgment. Nevertheless, while no society on earth can fully express this justice, the one that is more influenced by Christians and Christian teaching will more perfectly reflect a just society. For this reason Christians have a duty toward government.

The Church and the City of God

The relation between the church and the city of God is similar to the relation between the state and the city of man. They must not be confused. The church is not the city of God as such. The universal church contains both the wheat and the tares; it has people in it who belong to both the city of God and the city of man. The real church is the *communis sanctorum*—the body of the elect. Many of the elect are in the church, but some are not. Nevertheless, the church is the symbolic representative of the *civitas terrena* (the city of God on earth).

It is in Augustine's view of the church, particularly within the complex context in which he develops it, that the transformational character of his understanding of Christ and culture begins to emerge. Augustine is not so conscious a transformationalist as either Calvin or the liberation theologians we will study further on in this chapter. Nevertheless, he leaves us a legacy that is quickly developed into a transformational model. This legacy includes five ideas that provided the foundation for a complex transformational model.

First, Augustine identifies the *civitas dei* as the elect. In this sense the city of God transcends the New Testament church and includes all God's people from the beginning of history, whether they belong to the visible church or not. He is much more universal than Cyprian, who insists that "he who has not the church for his mother has not God for his father." The real issue between Cyprian and Augustine is whether or not the church is pure, made up of believers only. Cyprian argues that it is. Augustine argues that it contains a mixture of saints and sinners, that is, redeemed and unredeemed.

Augustine nevertheless insists, and this is the second point, that the visible church is the kingdom of God on earth. "It follows," he writes, "that the church even now is the Kingdom of Christ and the Kingdom of heaven. And so even now his saints reign with him, though not in the same way they will then reign; and yet the tares do not reign with him, although they are growing in the church side by side with the wheat."[7]

The third idea is that the Millennium is not a *future* reign of God but that the church is now in the Millennium. "In the meantime," he writes, "while the devil is bound for a thousand years, the saints reign with Christ, also for a thousand years; which are without doubt to be taken in the same sense, and as denoting the same period, that is, the beginning with Christ's first coming."[8]

The fourth point is that, given the facts that the church is the kingdom of God and that the period between Christ's first coming and second coming is the Millennium, the church is now the *regnum dei*, the rule of God. God is now ruling in His world through the church. In this respect Augustine interprets Revelation 20:4 ("then I saw thrones, and seated on them were those to whom judgment was committed") as "the seats of the authorities by whom the church is now governed, and those sitting on them as the authorities themselves." Consequently he concludes that "the best interpretation of the judgment given is that referred to in the words: 'whatever you bind on earth shall be bound in heaven; and whatever you loose on earth will be loosed in heaven'" (Matt. 18:18).[9] (Matt. 18:18).

The fifth point is clear from the preceding four: Augustine believes that the church assumes the shape of a society. But this idea emerged not so much through theological or philosophical speculation as through practical implication. The occasion for this emergence of the view of the church as a society was the contest with the Donatists.

The challenge that the Donatists offered the Catholics was in the area of ecclesiology. They claimed to be the true church. The issue for Augustine, at least in part, was the unity and peace of the church and the Roman Empire. To preserve unity and peace, Augustine turned to the state and developed an argument in favor of force in religious matters. He based it on the words of Christ "compel them to come in." Penalty, he argued, was useful because it helped one to reflect on error, turn away from it, and embrace the truth. It was, one might argue, persecution for the sake of good. The state, then, was called upon by Augustine to use force as a means of extending the kingdom. The state was in the service of the church.

All these ideas and the context in which they were developed tended in the words of John Figgis,

> to develop a state of mind which will picture the *civitas dei* as a Christianized Church-State, from which unbelievers are excluded, and which would claim, directly or indirectly, the supreme power in that state for the leaders of the hierarchy. If we add to this the effects of the church's long continuance in concentration upon earthly activities, the development of vast administrative machinery, the fact that she became to the conquering barbarians the symbol and the source of all culture, we are well on our way to such a conception of church-power as was represented by Innocent III.[10]

The Implications of De Civitate Dei *for the Medieval Era*

It is generally recognized that Augustine himself did not develop his thought into a far-reaching transformational approach.[11] Although he saw the vision of a culture under God, he did not see the implications of this *on earth* in the same way that his students of the medieval era did. Several examples must suffice to illustrate the point.

A shift in emphasis is noticeable in the thought of Pope Gelasius (492–96). He attempted to make the relation between kingly and priestly power more clear. In a letter to the Eastern emperor Anastasius he wrote, "Two there are, august emperor, by which this world is chiefly ruled, the sacred authority of the priesthood and the royal power. Of these the responsibility of the priests is more weighty in so far as they will answer for the kings of men themselves at the divine judgment."[12] This declaration, which appears over and over again during the controversies between king and pope in the medieval period, throws the weight of governing power over the world toward the church. For our purposes it is important to see the growing conviction of a single Christian society that includes within it the arm of the state and the arm of the church.

This sense of a Christianized society was central to the thinking of Charlemagne, who aimed for a unified realm in which Christ was King and all the earth was subject to Him. As a reader of Augustine, he envisioned a Christian empire, the city of God on earth. Both he and Otto after him sought to create an empire that was holy and Roman. Theirs was a calling to create a Catholic commonwealth with two swords governing the secular and sacred life of their inhabitants.

It was their hope, as well as the hope of Innocent III, to organize all of human life under God. The vision was for the church and the commonwealth to become one. The kingdom of God on earth was like a great church-state.

This quest for the "universal synthesis," the ultimate transformation of society by church, broke down in the fourteenth and fifteenth centuries but continued in a modified form in the thought of John Calvin. We turn now to his understanding of Christ and culture as the second example of a transformational viewpoint.

JOHN CALVIN

One of the major changes that occurred during the upheaval of the sixteenth century was the final breakdown of the medieval church-state synthesis. By the sixteenth century and especially after the Reformation movements were solidly under way, it was obvious that a unified world society under the church and state was no longer a possibility. Nevertheless, the idea of the unity of church and society in small units such as a nation, a territory, or even a city continued. Among the Reformers, only the Anabaptists broke with this conception, advocating complete separation between church and state. In order to understand Calvin's view of the Christian in culture, we must remember that he comes out of this milieu and thus presupposes a kind of unity between church and state. For Calvin, both those who govern in the church and those who govern in the state are called to function *under* the Word of God. With this thought in mind, we begin our study of Calvin by examining the principles that are basic to his understanding of the Christian in culture.

Calvin was the most formidable theologian of the sixteenth century and is without question one of the major theological thinkers in church history. Although his system of thought is highly complex and cannot be adequately summarized by a few key thoughts, we can at least see the foundations of his thinking about Christians in culture by looking at what he says on these four major themes: the sovereignty of God; the authority of Scripture; man, sin, and salvation; and the church.

In the first place, Calvin insists on the absolute sovereignty of God. In short, this means that God superintends the entirety of the world He has created. Calvin insists that God is not only Creator but also "a Governor and Preserver, and that not by producing a kind of general motion in the machine of the globe as well as in each of its parts, but by a special providence sustaining, cherishing, superintending, all the things which He has made, to the very minutest, even to a sparrow."[13] God's sovereignty extends to every phase of human life, not just man's personal and devotional life.

One immediate application of this view of sovereignty may be seen in Calvin's insistence that religion and culture are unified. If God is sovereign over His entire creation, then there can be no compartmentalization of religion. Religion is not something private and personal that runs alongside the rest of life. All of life and all of men's actions in life bear a religious character, because God is sovereign in every aspect of life. As Henry Van Til expresses it, "God's sovereignty is the atmosphere in which the Calvinist lives, the milieu in which he acts as a cultural being. It means that religion is not of life a thing apart, but the end-all and be-all of man's life under the sun."[14]

Another implication of God's sovereignty has to do with Christian calling and vocation. No aspect of life is outside God's concern and control. Because the world is not two domains—the one religious and the other profane—we should not act as though ministry in the church is a higher and holier calling than government service or any other form of work. All callings in life are directly related to God's purpose for creation, and the fulfillment of them is the carrying out of His will. Work in culture is therefore not a *may*, as though God permitted man to work in the "secular" world, but a *must*. All work is, for the Christian, a Christian vocation under the sovereign God.

How our life under the sovereign God is carried out is set forth in the second theme: man is to carry out his calling in absolute obedience to the authority of Scripture. Christianity is a world view encompassing all of life. For that reason Scripture is more than an authoritative guide for the way of salvation. It sets forth an authoritative interpretation of reality as a whole. As Van Til remarks, "In scripture the origin, nature, and goal of the world, man's habitat, and of man as image-bearer of God, are set forth. God's Word, then, is not merely a corrective, but it is regulative; its basic principles must become constitutive elements in a Calvinistic cultural philosophy."[15]

At the heart of Scripture is the third key to understanding Calvin's view of culture: the doctrine of man, sin, and salvation. Man is made in God's image, and as image-bearer he has a divine calling to do God's will in creation. As image-bearer, man is a social being and finds his fulfillment in life through relationships with others, particularly in marriage, in the family, and in his work. Within these relationships man has the opportunity to do the will of God and to express in concrete and tangible ways his obedience to the Creator.

But the Fall, which is man's choice not to do the will of God, demonstrated that man's ultimate affection and commitment were not toward God but toward himself. Rather than being a slave to God's will (which would be good for man, since God's will is for man's good), man becomes a slave to those passions and desires that tend to pervert his character as image-bearer. Consequently, man does himself a disservice. He becomes less human. He no longer lives up to the image of his original creation. He is less than what he could be.

The consequences of this perversion of the self-image are expressed in man's social relationships. Since marriage, family, and work are integral to man's being, they cannot escape the effect of man's decision to turn from the will of God. Biéler in his work entitled *The Social Humanism of Calvin* comments:

> Thinking to save his liberty, man has separated himself from God, thereby not only destroying his individual self but also changing the nature of social relationships. Man has distorted social life and economic exchanges. Thinking to find his freedom outside God, man in fact ends by foundering in a combination of slaveries. He becomes a slave of his own nature, of his sexual and emotional life, and of his work. He becomes the tyrant of his neighbor each time that he avoids being his neighbor's slave. All natural hierarchies are corrupted.[16]

But Calvin is no pessimist. The situation is not hopeless, for a new man has appeared. Jesus Christ is not only the Son of God but also the true man. He perfectly reflects the image of the Father. What this means for man is a new beginning—for him and therefore for his culture. Faith in Christ changes man—converts him. As a result, man no longer looks to himself or to his own will as the basis of his life but now looks outward toward God and puts himself under the authority of the Word of God. He becomes submissive to Christ and through him to the will of God. He now more perfectly bears the image of God.

The consequence of this change in man is a change in social relationships. And this brings us to the fourth of the four major themes of Calvin: the church. This small society exists in the midst of the larger society as, in the words of Biéler, "the small priming for the social restoration of humanness."[17] In a sense the church "is the embryo of an entirely new world where the once perverted social relations find anew their original nature."[18] This restoration of a new society is still fragmentary, of course, because of the persistence of sin in the life of the Christian.

An example of the shape this restoration takes within the church may be seen in Calvin's concern for the poor. Calvin insisted that an aspect of spiritual fellowship was the sharing of material goods. He felt strongly enough about this to organize the deaconship for the express purpose of redistributing the material goods of the church to those in need. This was a much more active side of church life in Calvin's day than it has been in twentieth-century churches within the Calvinistic tradition. However, in recent years there has been a renewed concern for the poor of the community and the world in some Calvinistic churches.

What Calvin says on these four themes, then—the sovereignty of God; the authority of Scripture; and the doctrines of man, sin and salvation, and the church—provides us with the biblical and theological keys to Calvin's view of the Christian in culture. We now turn to his thoughts on the role of the Christian in politics, in economics, and in work.

The Christian in Politics

We have seen that Calvinism is a world view: it sees all aspects of life as being under the sovereignty of God and under His Word. Let us see what this means in the political order.

Mueller comments, "The church and the state are both subject to the sovereign rule of God, *the regnum Dei et Christi.* The authority of both spheres inheres in the will and purpose of the living God."[19]

Although the origin of the state ultimately lies in the will of God, who decreed it into existence, we may speak of three earthly reasons for the state's existence. First, the fact of sin: because sin expresses itself in man's desire to develop culture away from the will of God, the state as an institution that holds sin in check has been instituted by God. Second, the goodness of God: the creation of the state may be seen as an act of God's goodness toward man. Sin unchecked by some external restraint would destroy man. Hence the third reason: the preservation of human life.

These reasons for the origin of the state suggest the purpose of the state. Calvin writes that its purpose is "to foster and maintain the external worship of God, to defend sound doctrine and the condition of the church, to adapt our conduct to human society, to form our manners to civil justice, to conciliate us to each other, to cherish common peace and tranquility."[20] He insists that magistrates have "a commission from God, that they are invested with divine authority, and in fact, represent the person of God, as whose substitutes they in a manner act."[21] Consequently, they are the "ordained guardians and vindicators of public innocence, modesty, honour, and tranquility, not that it should be their only study to provide for the common peace and safety."[22]

Both the origin and purpose of the state in Calvin's thought point to the necessity of Christian involvement. The effect of the involvement of Christians in government is obvious. If the Christian submits to what he understands the will of God to be in the state, the order of society will be stable and sin will be held in check. Involvement in government is therefore a Christian calling.

In this respect the church as a body has a particular role to play toward the state. In the first place, the church ought to be "a leaven inspiring and generating social, political, and economic life."[23] A dead church will make no impact on society. But a church that is alive to the Spirit, one that is constantly being regenerated by the Word of God, will be acting redemptively toward the social order.

Second, the church therefore has a kind of reforming role to play toward the state. W. Fred Graham sets forth four tasks that Calvin enumerates for the church in regard to the state. These all have to do with a kind of continuing reform of the church. The church is called upon to "pray for the political authorities." It is to "encourage the state to defend the poor and weak against the rich and powerful." The church must also "ensure its own status by calling on the political authorities for help in promoting true religion and even enforcing ecclesiastical discipline." And finally, the church has a responsibility "to warn the authorities when they are at fault."[24]

In order that the relation between church and state may work properly, Christians within the church must be obedient to the state. Obedience to the rulers is willed by God, for God has instituted the offices of the state. Furthermore, obedience is pleasing to God and helps to maintain the order and tranquillity of society, which brings glory to God.

Nevertheless, there are times when Christians have the right and duty to resist the state. Whenever the state demands something that opposes the will of God, the Christian has the right to resist compliance. The point is that the absolute authority over the Christian is Jesus Christ. For this reason, his obedience to the government is always conditional. But Calvin never teaches a radical revolutionary stance. He does not believe that it is right to uproot the social order. What Calvin does advocate is a prophetic witness that takes a firm stand for truth and justice but does not seek to take matters into its own hands. God himself will sooner or later deal with evil rulers.

The Christian and Economics

To assess Calvin's view of economics, we must remember that economic life and social life in his day were in upheaval. A rapidly growing capitalism had the effect of increasing the cost of living while at the same time decreasing the value of human labor. Consequently, a few were able to amass large fortunes while the masses were burdened with an increasing poverty.

Because Calvin did not separate the world into the secular and sacred domains, he was able to take the attitude that material goods belong to God. His positive attitude toward material possessions may be seen in what he thought about money. As Bieler points out, for Calvin "money is a sign with a two fold meaning: it is a sign of grace for him who through faith acknowledges that all his possessions come to him from God, but it is also a sign of condemnation of him who gets the goods of his living without discerning that they are the gift of God."[25]

Calvin believed in a mutual communication of goods. His model was the redistribution of the manna among the people of Israel as well as Paul's statement that "he who gathered much had nothing over, and he who gathered little had no lack" (2 Cor. 8:15). Calvin did not oppose the unequal distribution of goods as such. Instead, he advocated that the function of this unequal distribution was to provoke the redistribution of goods from the rich to the poor. The motive for this circulation of goods is the Christian persuasion of love. Anyone who really loves cannot be selfish. Thus the rich man actually has a mission to the poor. He is to share his wealth so that the poor will no longer be poor and the rich will no longer be rich. By the same token, however, the poor man has a mission to the rich: he provides the opportunity for the rich man to rid himself of his wealth and therefore free himself from becoming a slave to it. Unfortunately, however, the sinfulness of man expressed in his greed prevents the balance from occurring and maintains and encourages an inequality in society.

In the heart of sinful man, money becomes his god. Satan persuades man that money, not God, is what assures him of his daily bread. Furthermore, Satan persuades man that there are two domains—the secular and the religious—and that man can serve money in the secular domain so long as he serves God in the heart and in devotional practice. Consequently, both society and the church become perverse. By failing to speak out against the service of money, the church fails to fulfill its prophetic role within society. As a result, the evils produced by the worship of money rage on unchecked.

The answer to this unfortunate situation is found in the voluntary poverty of Jesus Christ and in the common grace of God, by which the goods of creation are meant to be freely dispersed to all. But it is the church that must put this into practice. For it is God's people who have a proper understanding of money and its use in society. The act of sharing, then, is essentially a spiritual act. By giving his goods for redistribution, man dethrones money and puts it into proper focus and use.

The rediscovery of the proper use of money has immediate social repercussions. The church rediscovers the spiritual nature of the mutual communication of goods. And through its obedience to the will of God in this respect, the church is able to point the way toward an economic equilibrium. For this reason Calvin instituted the deaconship and stressed the importance of giving and sharing in the Christian church.

Calvin also insisted that the state has a responsibility to the poor. It is the state's task to "guard against business interests milking the life of the people by unjust methods" as well as to guard itself against becoming an "economic liability to its citizens."[26]

The Christian and Work

Calvin's view of work, like his view of other aspects of life, is rooted in the will of the sovereign God. Work is not a meaningless activity, for it is the doing of the will of God in His creation. It is the means through which God's mandate for the maintenance and the unfolding of His creation is accomplished. As Bieler states, "The work of man has a meaning because, when rightly accomplished, it is the very work of God by which God supports the life of his creatures."[27]

Like everything else, however, work is affected by sin. It now participates in the chaos introduced into the created order. Man has freed himself from doing the will of God and seeks instead to work autonomously. His activity therefore produces pain, disruption, inequality, injustice, and the like.

In order to restore work to its original meaning, man must be realigned with Jesus Christ and through Him brought back to obedience to the will of God.

For Calvin, the Sabbath as a day of rest points to the recovery of the meaning of work. Rest in and of itself has no meaning; its purpose is to put man back into the condition of being able to work. In the freedom of rest our minds and bodies are able to recognize again the Creator and our relationship to Him. To misuse the Sabbath by not observing it as a day of rest results in the corruption of work.

Because man is created to work, all forms of idleness are a curse. To be lazy, or to accumulate wealth through the sweat of another man's brow, represents a rupture with God and His calling for man in work. Consequently, unemployment is a social scourge to be fought against, "for to deprive man of his work is truly a crime. As a matter of fact, it is equivalent to taking away his life."[28] To abuse another person in his work or to exploit workers is also a crime.

Since work is doing the will of God, all men ought to recognize that pay is the result of the grace of God. This means that both rich and poor alike receive their wage from God. Therefore for an employer to withhold an employee's fair share is to withhold from him what God has paid him. "The master," as Graham points out, "is simply 'paymaster' for the heavenly master."[29]

The real point is that everything belongs to God and man. Whether he is an employer or an employee, a person is simply a steward of God's creation. And since man lives in a solidarity with his fellow man, he must remember that there is one "master" over all—God. Salary must be seen, then, to use Biéler's words, "in relation to the real needs of the working man considered in their new dignity as children of God. This does not forbid, but on the contrary, it commands the state to exercise a certain control over salaries. Salaries must be guaranteed by contractual regulations. Finally, in case of conflicts, one must recur to arbitrations."[30]

All of this must be seen in the context of Calvin's world view. Because this is God's world, the purpose of economic goods and work is the service of God in society. What serves the best interests of society in terms of fairness and equal distribution of goods serves God. What creates an imbalance in society and produces poverty and suffering does not serve God. Commerce, then, "must relieve the pain of man and render his existence pleasant. In order to respond to the purpose of God, commerce always must tend to this goal."[31] goal."[31]

LIBERATION THEOLOGY

Liberation theology is one of the fastest-growing and perhaps one of the most influential modern ideas having to do with the relation between Christianity and society. The context from which the idea of liberation emerged may be first located in the Bandung Conference of 1955, which promoted the concept of the "Third World." Since then the term has come to mean those areas and people that are associated with neither the capitalist nor the communist system—the countries commonly known as "underdeveloped." The Bandung Conference called the world to attend to these people and countries and to aid them in their self-development.

In response to this appeal, many developed countries as well as many church denominations and organizations became heavily involved in the Third World. Technical aid and personnel were made available, and a noble attempt was made to help struggling countries get on their feet.

Disillusionment soon set in, however, because the expected social and economic changes did not occur. The poor nations were becoming poorer. The conditions of human life, far from being bettered, were gradually becoming worse.

In this context arose what one commentator describes as "a cry that what was needed was the *liberation of persons and peoples to be the subject of their own history* rather than the objects of someone else's history, whether benignly or selfishly conceived."[32] Dependence on other nations and their technical expertise was not what was needed. The answer lay instead in liberation.

At this point, at least, the church was seen to stand on the side of the oppressor. The native church, it seemed, stood on the side of the oppressive regimes. And the foreign churches came hand in hand with the imperialistic policies of their home nations.

In the meantime the clergy, particularly those who worked with the poor, became more and more critical of the church and supportive of the demands being made for change. This pressure prompted five conferences in 1970, all of which (both Catholic and Protestant) produced a number of significant papers and statements calling the church to an active position in the struggle for justice and economic opportunity among the poor. Gradually the concept of liberation became more clear in the context of theological and practical analysis and articulation.

A Definition of Liberation Theology

Liberation theology is rooted in the concern for salvation. Salvation is seen as something intended not merely or exclusively for the "soul" of man but for the whole man, the whole created order. Liberation theologians want to see Christ's redemptive work applied to the whole man, liberating him from all those forces—personal, social, moral, political, economic, and otherwise—that deny him the experience of being free to enjoy the benefits of salvation in every aspect of life.

Consequently liberation theology is confrontational theology. It confronts evil in all its expressions—personal and social—and demands *release* from the power of evil. But it does not confront evil from the outside. It is not as though it were church versus society, for there is only one history, and what is done to bring about release must be done within the framework of that history. Thus liberation theology identifies the continuing act of salvation with the very process of history, which is the context of both oppression and liberation. The liberation theologian Gustavo Gutierrez puts it this way:

> Liberation emphasizes that man transforms himself by conquering his liberty throughout his existence and his history. The Bible presents liberation-salvation-in-Christ as the total gift, which, by taking on the levels we indicate, gives the whole process of liberation its deepest meaning and its complete and unforeseeable fulfillment. Liberation can thus be approached as a single salvific process. This viewpoint, therefore, permits us to consider the *unity, without confusion,* of man's various dimensions, that is, his relationships with other men and with the Lord.[33]

To try to understand this definition more fully and to relate liberation theology to the problem of the church in society, we will examine four issues that liberation theology poses: (1) the nature of salvation, (2) the historical dimension of salvation, (3) the political dimension of salvation, and (4) the church in the world.

The Nature of Salvation

Liberation theology rejects the notion of the "saved" and the "unsaved." That the church represents the "saved" and that the mission of the church in the world is to "save the pagans" is replaced by the idea of the universality of God's will to save. God has, through Christ, saved and redeemed the world. The redemption of Christ is so far-reaching that we can regard the whole cosmic order as saved. Salvation is therefore not something that is "other-worldly"; it has to do with this life now and may be defined as "the communion of men with God and the communion of men among themselves."[34] The emphasis is not so much on "God did something that you must believe" or "because of Christ God has changed His attitude toward you." Rather, the emphasis falls on the cosmic redemption that took place in history and has immediate implications for man in his life now.[35]

Biblically, this understanding of salvation is already set forth in the Exodus event. The Exodus, properly understood, is a re-creation. That is, the Exodus brings creation and redemption together. It emphasizes that God reveals Himself in history and that His salvation takes place through historical events. Creation is the beginning of God's salvation because it initiates history, the context in which God's saving work actually takes place. The source for this vision is the liberation of the children of Israel from their bondage in Egypt.

The liberation of Israel was not only historical but also political. Not only were they called *away from* a situation of bondage, misery, and injustice, but they were also called *to* the task of constructing a just society. They were thus breaking with an old order and creating a new one. "The Exodus is the long march towards the promised land in which Israel can establish a society free from misery and alienation."[36] In this sense the Exodus is a re-creation. It is a new beginning.

Like the Exodus, the redemptive work of Jesus Christ is a new beginning and is presented in the context of Creation. Paul affirms that "in him all things were created" and that "in him all the fulness of God was pleased to dwell, and through him to reconcile to himself all things, whether on earth or in heaven, making peace by the blood of his cross" (Col. 1:15-20). The work of Christ is also a liberation from sin and all its consequences. As the Exodus inaugurated a new people, so too the Cross marks a new beginning. It calls into existence a new people who are called to continue the work of creation and redemption through their labor and involvement in life. Gustavo Gutierrez summarizes this notion well:

> Consequently, when we assert that man fulfills himself by continuing the work of creation by means of his labor, we are saying that he places himself, by this very fact, within an all-embracing salvific process. To work, to transform this world, is to become a man and to build the human community; it is also to save. Likewise, to struggle against misery and exploitation and to build a just society is already to be part of the saving action, which is moving towards its complete fulfillment. All this means that building the temporal city is not simply a stage of "humanization" or "pre-evangelization" as was held in theology up until a few years ago. Rather it is to become part of a saving process which embraces the whole of man and all human history. Any theological reflection òn human work and social praxis ought to be rooted in this fundamental affirmation.[37]

Salvation is therefore not only that which looks back to Creation and re-creates in the present but also that which looks beyond the present into the future. Biblical religion is a religion of promise. Salvation has to do with the progressive unfolding of that promise within history. It is already partially fulfilled in historical events, but it is not completely fulfilled. Therefore it is constantly projecting itself into the future as a historical reality that is in the process of being fulfilled. This process is happening now as mankind struggles for a just society.

The Historical Dimension of Salvation

To begin with, liberation theology strongly emphasizes the historical nature of the Christian faith. Not only did God create the world, and by that initiate human history, but He also entered into human history as a man. Therefore it is in human history that we encounter God.[38]

In the Bible the entrance of God into history is expressed in a twofold process. First, the presence of God is "universalized" and, second, His presence is "internalized." Let us see what liberation theologians mean by these two terms.

Scripture reveals a gradual universalization of the presence of God. To begin with, God reveals His presence within history on the mountain. At Sinai, as He entered into a covenant with the people, He was somewhat distant from them. Gradually, however, He entered more and more into the life of the people. His presence was made known in the tent, then in the ark of the covenant, and finally in the temple. While the tent and the ark were mobile, the temple was localized. To counteract the idea that God could be contained, the prophets emphasized the theme that God's dwelling place was in the heavens. In this way they opposed those who wished to externalize and localize the presence of God.

In the New Testament God's presence became a reality in the person of Jesus Christ—"the Word became flesh." In the Incarnation God irreversibly committed Himself to human history. The historical nature of God's presence in the world does not stop there, however, for the Christian community, called by Christ, is His body in the world. Each Christian, as Paul taught, is a temple of the Holy Spirit; the presence of God is within every Christian. That is not all, however. According to Gutierrez, "Not only is the Christian a temple of God; every man is."[39] The presence of God has, then, in Scripture, gradually extended from "the mountain" to "every man." God's presence is universalized in history in every man.

Secondly, the presence of God has gradually undergone an internalization. A glance at biblical history suggests that God's initial relationship with men was somewhat external. He came to them in the mountain, then in the tent, later in the ark, then in the temple, and finally in a man. The constant problem in the Old Testament was the tendency to externalize the worship of God and obedience to Him. The prophets recognized this failure and insisted that the day would come when a mere external relationship to God would be replaced by an internal commitment to Him. "A new heart I will give you, and a new spirit I will put within you; and I will take out of your flesh the heart of stone and give you a heart of flesh" (Ezek. 36:26). With the coming of God into human history and the establishment of the new covenant, the presence of God is transferred from external signs and integrated within the human heart. God is now within man!

This dual process in which God's presence is made real in history and integrated within man is accomplished in Jesus Christ. He is the focal point for this reality. For this reason spirituality can no longer be separated from materiality and human history. Spirituality is expressed within the concrete events of life and through people. This material nature of spirituality is pointed up by certain biblical themes. Two in particular are the emphasis on *doing* justice and the teaching that Christ is to be found in one's neighbor. The emphasis on doing justice is central to the preaching of the prophets. It is clear from their teaching that to exploit the weak and poor is to commit an offense against God (Prov. 17:5), while to act with fairness and justice toward the poor and oppressed is to love God (Jer. 22:13-16). The same point is made by Jesus in the parable of the good Samaritan. The point, though, is not solely that one *does* justice but that concern for others grows out of charity. Paul teaches in 1 Corinthians 13 that all actions that do not grow out of charity are empty. God's presence in man is not a mere objective rule over man that creates a sense of obligation within him; rather, the presence of God's love within man motivates him to be charitable.[40]

Man's charity, however, is not a mere wishful desire for the well-being of others. Rather, it is a charity, like that of Jesus, that manifests itself within the structures of society. As Gutierrez explains it,

> Charity is today a "political charity," according to the phrase of Pius XII. Indeed to offer food or drink in our day is a political action; it means the transformation of a society structured to benefit a few who appropriate to themselves the value of the work of others. This transformation ought to be directed

toward a radical change in the foundation of society, that is, the private ownership of the means of production.[41]

This statement leads us from the historical dimension of salvation to its necessary correlative, the political dimension.

The Political Dimension of Salvation

The notion of liberation is complex, and we must differentiate among three levels of meaning. The first is political and refers to a real and effective political action; the second is utopian and refers to the projection of history; and the third is on the level of faith and refers to the re-creation of the world effected by the work of Christ. Although these levels may be treated as distinct, they are profoundly linked together by salvation, which both destroys the old order and establishes the new. Political action, then, within the context of salvation is the path that man cuts out in history toward his own future. It runs between the old order and the new.

The political dimension of salvation presupposes sin. Sin, "a breach of friendship with God and others,"[42] is a reality within the structures of society. Consequently, as Paul suggests in Romans 8, the whole cosmos suffers as a result of sin. All violence, greed, hate, injustice, suppression, and oppression that occur in society are results of sin. And the creation is struggling to escape this sin, to become liberated into the new order.

Although it is Christ who, by the redemption He has provided, has freed man and the creation from the bondage of sin, it is now the responsibility of man as lord of His creation and co-participant in the historical process of redemption to work toward the realization of salvation. This process begins with a rejection: man is called to reject sin in all its forms. This rejection takes place within the Creation as man takes hold of his own destiny and confronts sin, the ultimate root of all injustice and exploitation. Faith, because it looks to the future, recognizes that the confrontation with sin is not vain, for God calls man to it and assures him of ultimate victory. In this confrontation, history becomes "a thrust into the future." And within this forward movement of history man is committed to the creation of a just society and finally to a new man.[43]

The gospel is therefore not a merely private faith; it is one that makes a deep social impact on man and his culture. The political nature of the gospel is not a mere appendage but resides at the very heart of its message. Because the gospel proclaims a "new creation," it takes on Israel's hope and gives it its deepest meaning. It reveals the hope of a just society and calls society to follow unexplored paths and open itself to a society of brotherhood and justice, where communion with God and men can become a reality. In this way the political dimension of salvation is made a reality through the work of the church in the world.

The Church in the World

The meaning of the church is clear only when it is set within the plan of salvation. Since the work of salvation is a reality that occurs within history and since the church is an entity within history, an expression of that salvation is to be found within the church.

The church, then, may be defined as the visible sign of God's saving work. It is not something that exists for itself, rather, it exists for others. Its identity, because it is rooted in the work of Christ, is found outside itself in relation to the reality of the kingdom that it announces.

The church therefore has the responsibility to signify in its own internal structure the salvation it announces. It is in that sense a place of liberation. In the church the break with an unjust order occurs. For the church is the people of God who live in history oriented toward the future promised by Christ. The church's faithfulness to the gospel leaves it no alternative except, as a visible sign of the presence of the Lord, to aspire to liberation in the struggle for a more humane and just society.

The church signifies this liberation from within in two ways: in the eucharistic celebration and in the creation of brotherhood.

The first task of the church is to celebrate the death and resurrection of Jesus, which accomplished God's saving action in the world. The Eucharist in its original form is celebrated against the background of the Jewish Passover and all that this means in regard to the Israelites' liberation from Egypt. It signifies the passing over from death to life. It points to the liberation from sin and the ultimate communion with God. In this way the Eucharist goes to the heart of liberation, for it points to the destruction of sin and beyond to the ultimate communion with God.

This eucharistic celebration is closely linked to the creation of brotherhood. For one thing, the Eucharist is celebrated within the context of a meal, a common sign of brotherhood. Therefore, the Eucharist points to and is basic to the experience of brotherhood. Brotherhood, as Gutierrez points out, means three things. First, it has to do with the common ownership of goods (Acts 2:44; 4:32); second, it points to the union Christians experience with Christ through the Eucharist (1 Cor. 10:16); and third, it ultimately speaks to the union Christians have with the Father (1 John 1:6). Consequently, "the basis for brotherhood is full communion with the persons of the Trinity. The bond which unites God and man is celebrated—that is, effectively recalled and proclaimed—in the Eucharist."[44]

Second, the church signifies liberation outside itself in its functions of denunciation and annunciation.

In its denunciation the church must make its position toward social injustice clear. It must undertake, as Gutierrez explains it, "a prophetic *denunciation* of every dehumanizing situation, which is contrary to brotherhood, justice, and liberty. At the same time it must criticize every sacralization of oppressive structures to which the church itself might have contributed."[45] The best way for the church to achieve this is to cast its lot with the oppressed and the exploited in their struggle for a just society, even if this means being critical of itself and of its own economic security—which may contribute to the problem.

The *annunciation* of the gospel consists not so much in words as in living. The church must live what it proclaims. Says Gutierrez, "The annunciation of the gospel thus has a conscienticizing function, or in other words, a politicizing function. But this is made real and meaningful only by living and announcing the gospel from within a commitment to liberation, only in concrete, effective solidarity with people and exploited social classes."[46]

A most significant way in which the church can live its proclamation is in its involvement with the class struggle. Humanity is divided into oppressors and the oppressed. The struggle to be free takes place in the context of the economic, social, political, and cultural realm. The church cannot be neutral to this struggle. Neither can it reject the class struggle; otherwise it perpetuates the division of society. In the midst of this struggle the church's calling is to lead society toward the eschatological vision of the kingdom. In this way and through this means society will become transformed as the future becomes a present reality.

CONCLUSION

We have seen that the concerns of the transformational model are rooted in both Scripture and church history. Although the three examples we have studied are quite far apart in the specifics of their application, they have certain common features that we may conclude are characteristic of the transformational model:

1. *The central conviction of the transformational model is that the structures of life can be converted and changed.* For this reason we can conclude that the transformational model is generally activistic and optimistic. It believes that the kingdom of God can be experienced to a degree in this world.

2. *The transformational model presupposes the radical effect of sin on all the structures of life.* Sin is not seen as something merely personal or private. Instead, the permeating effect of sin within all of life is recognized. Man's sinful nature is reflected and enlarged in his cultural unfolding.

3. *The transformational model presupposes the cosmic nature of Christ's redemption.* The redemption of Christ is far-reaching. It is personal, but it is much more, for it extends into every area of man's life in the world. It has to do with the restoration of the world and of man to the original intent of God.

4. *The transformational model sees the church as that social context in which the redeemed reality is to be modeled.* The church is more than a mere collection of believers. It is a new community called to exemplify the principles of the kingdom and thus to have a saving effect on all the structures of life.

Questions for Discussion

1. Scan this chapter and write down all those words and terms that are unfamiliar to you. Define them in your own words. What do these ideas have to do with the Christian in culture?
2. Compare the transformationalist with the separatist and identifier. Which are you?
3. Is the Augustinian vision of the transformation of society a viable option today?
4. Do you think that Calvin's view of church and state is a viable option today?
5. Would you be willing to follow Calvin's view of economics? His view of work?
6. If you were a member of the poor class in Latin America would you support liberation theology?
7. List ten ways you can work to transform society.

Further Reading

Augustine. *The City of God.* Edited by David Knowles. Baltimore: Penguin, 1972.
Baldwin, Marshall W. *The Medieval Church.* Ithaca: Cornell University, 1963.

Bieler, Andre. *The Social Humanism of Calvin.* Translated by Paul T. Fuhrmann. Richmond: John Knox, 1964.

Bonino, Jose Miguez. *Doing Theology in a Revolutionary Situation.* Philadelphia: Fortress, 1975.

Calvin, John. *Institutes of the Christian Religion.* 2 vols. Grand Rapids: Eerdmans, 1966.

Cochrane, Charles Norris. *Christianity and Classical Culture.* London: Oxford University, 1974.

Figgis, John Neville. *The Political Aspects of St. Augustine's City of God.* Gloucester: Peter Smith, 1963.

Goulet, Denis. *A New Moral Order.* Maryknoll, N.Y.: Orbis, 1974.

Graham, Fred W. *The Constructive Revolutionary: John Calvin, His Socio-Economic Impact.* Richmond: John Knox, 1971.

Gutierrez, Gustavo. *A Theology of Liberation.* Maryknoll, N.Y.: Orbis, 1973.

Lawrentin, Rene. *Liberation, Development and Salvation.* Translated by Charles Underhill Quinn. Maryknoll, N.Y.: Orbis, 1972.

Mueller, William A. *Church and State in Luther and Calvin.* Nashville: Broadman, 1954.

Soelle, Dorothee. *Political Theology.* Philadelphia: Fortress, 1974.

Tierney, Brian. *The Crisis of Church and State 1050-1300.* Englewood Cliffs: Prentice-Hall, 1964.

Van Til, Henry. *The Calvinistic Concept of Culture.* Philadelphia: Presbyterian and Reformed, 1959.

A
CONTEMPORARY
PERSPECTIVE

8

A Case for Evangelical Social Responsibility

I have rooted the case for social responsibility in both the Scriptures and Christian history, a combination that should be persuasive for Evangelicals. However, I admit that there are some loose ends, particularly in view of the vast differences in approach to social responsibility seen in our three historical models. For that reason I will argue the case more specifically from the viewpoint of evangelical history and theology and then draw some conclusions. I will treat this material in three parts: the historical case, the biblical-theological case, and a contemporary stance.

THE HISTORICAL CASE

The roots of modern-day evangelical Christianity are highly complex and diverse. Nevertheless, there is general agreement that evangelicalism was given shape by the nineteenth-century revivals in England and America. It is also recognized that these revivalistic fires account for the origins of the modern Christian social movements.

Social Change in England

Earle Cairns, an evangelical church historian, has described the sources of evangelical social reform:

> The social dynamic was mainly the result of revival after 1739. Social reform was not left to professional social workers or to sentimental crusaders. Such work was accepted as a calling of God by statesmen, such as Wilberforce and Shaftesbury. They had the backing of converted people whose Christianity was also expressed in political support of social change along Christian lines. . . . All classes were affected by the earlier Wesleyan and the later evangelical revivals.[1]

John Wesley, George Whitefield, and other leaders of the revival held what is known as a holistic view of salvation. They did not separate the body from the soul, the material from the spiritual, the personal from the social. Rather, their approach to revival stimulated the improvement of social conditions and the bettering of human life.

Wesley himself was in the forefront of social change. In 1746 he opened a free medical dispensary for the poor of Bristol, England. In 1785 he organized a Friends Society to aid strangers and those in need. He wrote against bribe-taking and smuggling. He supported the rise of education, particularly the Sunday school movement. He fought against the slave trade. He supported prison reform. And he freely gave his money for the support of these various reforms. It is estimated that he gave more than £30,000 during his lifetime to such causes.

Wesley was not unique. Many other Christians, including members of the upper classes such as wealthy politicians and businessmen from Clapham Commons, a village near London, were involved in social reform. Although they were nicknamed "the saints" by their opponents in Parliament, these benevolent Christians are better known as the Clapham sect. They gave away large portions of their income for the support of social change. Among them were William Wilberforce, who led the fight to stop slave trading, and Granville Sharp, who brought about the judicial decision in 1772 to free the slaves in England.

Among the numerous social movements that resulted from the influence and leadership of Evangelicals, we will look at three major ones: the abolition of slavery, prison reform, and the improvement of working conditions.

The abolition of slavery became the life interest of Granville Sharp (1735-1813), a grandson of the archbishop of Canterbury during the reign of Anne. His study of the Old Testament convinced him that slavery was a sin. Setting out to destroy this evil in England, he found out that he had the support of most of the clergy of the Church of England.

One of the many persons influenced by Sharp was William Wilberforce, a member of the Clapham sect, an Evangelical, and a member of Parliament. Wilberforce worked with other Evangelicals who gathered information for him and actively agitated in Parliament for the abolition of slavery. His move for abolition was defeated in 1792 and again in 1796. Rather than giving up, the Evangelicals became even more active in pressing for abolition. In 1802 they published the *Christian Observer*, an anti-slavery magazine that spread their ideas further and gained support for the cause. In 1804 Wilberforce introduced another bill for abolition, and it eventually passed.

But the abolitionists did not stop with their victory in England. They carried their cause to other countries and were influential in stopping the slave trade in Denmark, the United States, Sweden, Holland, and other countries.

The same kind of energy was put into prison reform. John Wesley and some of his fellow members of the Holy Club had visited prisoners in the jail at Oxford. From that time on Wesley took an interest in prisoners. He publicized the poor conditions in prisons and advocated reform. John Howard (1726-1790), who became the foremost leader in prison reform, freely acknowledged his indebtedness to Wesley. Howard, who had had experience in a jail in Portugal, sought, through the accumulation of evidence, to change the laws that treated prisoners unjustly. As a result of his work a number of improvements were made, including the development of fair laws, the ending of the unfair practice of jailors' fees, and the improvement of sanitary conditions.

Similar efforts were made to improve the lot of workers through changes in the laws. The most ardent champion of the working class was Anthony Shaftesbury, a committed Evangelical and a member of Parliament. Comments Cairns: "He was of the opinion that what was morally right must be politically right and what was morally wrong could never be politically right. He would use the law to restrain those who were vicious and to protect the oppressed."[2] Shaftesbury worked tirelessly for shorter hours, better working conditions, and better pay for workers. As a result of his spirit and leadership, laws were eventually passed that reduced the length of the working day, restricted and regulated the employment of women and children, and reformed such occupations as mining, chimney sweeping, and the operation of lodging houses.

All these changes came about because men and women had experienced the saving reality of Jesus Christ. The early Evangelicals understood the "cosmic" dimension of Christianity—that it extended to the whole of man and to his entire existence under the sun. Theirs was no reductionistic, anti-material, "soul-only" salvation.

Social Change in America

At the same time that these social changes were occurring in England, similar changes were being made in America, and for the same reason: revival. In an interesting book entitled *Discovering an Evangelical Heritage,* Donald Dayton looks back into the roots of his own denomination, the Wesleyan Methodist, and evangelicalism in general. Happily he discovered that his denomination "was a product of the closest parallel to the civil rights movement in American history—the abolitionist protest against slavery in the pre–Civil War period."[3] Further research led him into the "sweet irony that this denomination was not unique, but shared a reformist heritage with other aspects of Evangelicalism."[4] Dayton discusses some of the major reformers and movements that gave shape to an evangelical social conscience. Three persons— among many—who illustrate the social roots of evangelicalism are Jonathan Blanchard, Charles G. Finney, and Theodore Weld.

Jonathan Blanchard was the founder of Wheaton College. By today's standards he would be considered a radical. A plaque in Blanchard Hall on the Wheaton campus contains a quotation from an address by Blanchard entitled "A Perfect State of Society." The plaque reads: "Society is perfect where what is right in theory exists in fact; where practice coincides with principle, and the Law of God is the Law of the Land."

Blanchard did not separate his theology from practice. Unlike those who are concerned with right doctrine and a private ethic, Blanchard's concern was for right doctrine and a *public* ethic.

For example, the doctrine of man made in the image of God was not a matter for pure speculation for Blanchard; it was basic to his convictions against slavery. And it was not enough for him merely to have an anti-slavery position in his heart. Rather, his theological conviction gave rise to an active engagement within society against the evil institution of slavery. Blanchard worked against many odds—and with no little opposition from some Christians—to abolish slavery. His concern (and the motto he left for Wheaton College) was "For Christ and His Kingdom." By this he meant the rule of God in the life of society, which brought about a gradual transformation of culture.

This was also true of Charles G. Finney, another founding father of American evangelicalism. Although Finney is best remembered as a preaching evangelist, he also exercised a strong influence in America through his writing, particularly his *Lectures on Revivals of Religion.* In this work he argued that "revivals are hindered when ministers and churches take wrong ground in regard to any question involving human rights."[5] These were no idle words. Finney practiced what he preached in regard to slavery and insisted that the church

must face that issue. "One of the reasons for the low estate of
religion at the present time," he said, "is that many churches
have taken the wrong side on the subject of slavery, have
suffered prejudice to prevail over principle, and have feared to
call this abomination by its true name."[6]

Theodore Weld, converted under the ministry of Finney,
became the most important anti-slavery worker in America.
For some time after his conversion he worked in the "Holy
Band," a group of Finney's assistants. Throughout the years,
Weld continued to apply to social issues the principles taught
by Finney. He was a major influence in opening the door for
women to speak in mixed gatherings, which, says Dayton,
"foreshadowed the later practice of women taking to the platform in defense of abolitionism and the consequent birth of
feminism."[7] But his greatest work was done in the anti-slavery
movements, as recognized by the *Dictionary of American Biog-
raphy,* which calls Weld "the greatest of the abolitionists."

These examples illustrate the extensive nature of the
evangelical impulse as it took shape in the nineteenth century.
Evangelicalism in its best form is no stranger to social concern; such concern is, in fact, close to the center of what
evangelical Christianity is all about. But this does not seem to
be the case today. Instead, evangelicalism appears to be
aligned not only with conservative theology but also with conservative politics, and it is certainly not (as a whole) in the
forefront of social reform. Whatever happened to change the
movement so that the focus of social outreach is no longer on
encouraging constructive change but preserving the status
quo?

The Shift in Evangelicalism

During the past century, evangelicalism has undergone a
shift that is highly complex historically, theologically, and socially. The details of this change still lie buried in history.
Someday, perhaps, historians will be able to uncover them.[8]

One reason, of course, is the difficulty of maintaining any
movement for a long period of time. The dynamic of all

movements tends to atrophy and eventually die. The evangelical revivals of the nineteenth century were certainly not immune from this natural cycle.

Another reason may lie in the impact made by the Civil War, which threw cold water on the utopian hope for a world changed through the betterment of society. The war was a slice of realism interjected in the midst of many dreams. It had the effect of bringing people back into the reality of this world and thus it diluted the reformers' vision.

Another influence was the shift that occurred in eschatology. Nineteenth-century evangelicalism was largely optimistic and post-millennial. With the rise of dispensationalism, which accented not so much the vision of the kingdom as teaching about the end time, and with the catastrophe of wars and depression in the early twentieth century, evangelicalism shifted toward a pessimistic mood. It began to look for the "life beyond" as the better place and became less concerned about making this life better. The emphasis then fell on "rescuing" fallen souls from the sinking ship. Consequently, evangelism lost its social emphasis.

Since the 1960s, however, a renewed sense of the social implications of the gospel has begun to emerge within evangelical ranks. Among the causes for this change are a changing cultural climate, the demise of liberal social outreach, and the influence of a number of younger Evangelicals who have become social activists.

This trend found expression in a ground-breaking statement made by a group of Evangelicals who met in Chicago in 1973. They organized themselves as Evangelicals for Social Change and wrote the "Chicago Declaration," a far-reaching statement chiding Evangelicals with complicity in social evil and calling for an active and prophetic stance against social evils in North America. The statement reads:

> As evangelical Christians committed to the Lord Jesus Christ and the full authority of the Word of God, we affirm that God lays total claim upon the lives of His people. We cannot, therefore, separate our lives in Christ from the situation in which God has placed us in the United States and the world.

We confess that we have not acknowledged the complete claims of God on our lives.

We acknowledge that God requires love. But we have not demonstrated the love of God to those suffering social abuses.

We acknowledge that God requires justice. But we have not proclaimed or demonstrated His justice to an unjust American society. Although the Lord calls us to defend the social and economic rights of the poor and the oppressed, we have mostly remained silent. We deplore the historic involvement of the church in America with racism and the conspicuous responsibility of the evangelical community for perpetuating the personal attitudes and institutional structures that have divided the body of Christ along color lines. Further, we have failed to condemn the exploitation of racism at home and abroad by our economic system

We affirm that God abounds in mercy and that He forgives all who repent and turn from their sins. So we call our fellow evangelical Christians to demonstrate repentance in a Christian discipleship that confronts the social and political injustice of our nation.

We must attack the materialism of our culture and the maldistribution of the nation's wealth and services. We recognize that as a nation we play a crucial role in the imbalance and injustice of international trade and development. Before God and a billion hungry neighbors, we must rethink our values regarding our present standard of living and promote more just acquisition and distribution of the world's resources.

We acknowledge our Christian responsibilities of citizenship. Therefore, we must challenge the misplaced trust of the nation in economic and military might—a proud trust that promotes a national pathology of war and violence which victimizes our neighbors at home and abroad. We must resist the temptation to make the nation and its institutions objects of near-religious loyalty.

We acknowledge that we have encouraged men to prideful domination and women to irresponsible passivity. So we call both men and women to mutual submission and active discipleship.

We proclaim no new gospel, but the Gospel of our Lord Jesus Christ who, through the power of the Holy Spirit, frees people from sin so that they might praise God through works of righteousness.

By this declaration, we endorse no political ideology or party, but call our nation's leaders and people to that righteousness which exalts a nation.

We make this declaration in the Biblical hope that Christ is coming to consummate the Kingdom, and we accept His claim on our total discipleship till He comes.[9]

The Biblical-Theological Case

There are several presuppositions of evangelical Christianity that we need to keep in mind as we look at the biblical-theological basis for involvement in social issues. In the first place, Evangelicals presuppose *supernaturalism*. The world is not all there is. The meaning of the world is found in God; He is the giver of meaning. Evangelicalism is also *revelational*. The meaning of the world is discovered, not through some brilliant flash of insight, but through a communication from God Himself. This self-disclosure is preserved in Scripture as a trustworthy record of God's revelation. Furthermore, evangelicalism is *incarnational*. God came to man in the person of Jesus Christ in time, space, and history. Christ is more than a man; He is the God-man. This world has been visited by the supernatural. Because the emphasis is on this world, evangelicalism can also be referred to as *historical*. Christianity is not some ethereal or esoteric notion about life. Rather, it is a historical religion *par excellence*. It has gotten its hands dirty with the mud and filth of life. But to say that Christianity is historical is not to refer to the Old Testament and the early church alone. It is not as though God came to us and then left us to our own devices. His work in history continues in the church. And, finally, evangelicalism is also *Spirit-directed*. We cannot talk about the Christian faith without recognizing the role of the Spirit in making God present to the life of the church.

With these basic presuppositions in mind, we turn to the three-part schema of creation-sin-redemption as the basic biblical-theological framework supporting a case for evangelical social responsibility.

Creation

The early Fathers taught that the Son proceeds from the *nature* of the Father and the world resulted from an *act of the will of the Father*. This comparison throws into bold relief the Christian conviction that the world is not an extension of God, that it exists as something apart from God, and that it is nevertheless contingent upon God. One important implication of this view is the accent it places on history. Creation initiates history. And it is here, within history, that the purposes of God are worked out.

God is the fundamental reality of the entire created order and of everything that takes place in history. Therefore everything that is can be properly perceived only in relation to Him. The key that unlocks the door to the perception of God in creation and history is *purpose*. The world is an expression of God's purposes. The world is not a machine that works on its own. Rather, in its creation, in its providential ordering, and in its final goal, it is an expression of the purposeful activity of God. This purpose binds together in an inner connection the succession of events from beginning to end and thus gives meaning to the whole course of history.

This purposefulness of God is first evident in the creation of mankind. Because man is the image-bearer of God, he has a unique role to play in the created order. He has been given "dominion" over nature. His task in the world is "to till the garden," to unfold all of culture as the agent of God, the image-bearer.

This is a religious task. Man does not "have" a religion as something in addition to himself. Rather, by virtue of God's image within him and the task he is called to in the world, he is to live all of life "religiously." Man is the agent of God's purposes. He is to fulfill the purpose of God, to carry out His will within the created order.

For this reason man's religious activity must be seen within a historical dimension. That is, his activity as a religious person has historical consequences. Religion does not run alongside life or above life, as though it were some esoteric or ephemeral thing. It has to do with the very stuff of life itself and takes shape in the structures of family, state, education, work, play, and all other aspects of life because man is a being in history.

This certainly does not mean that we cannot talk of man as a spiritual being. What it means is that we refuse to separate the spiritual from the material. The material is not all that is. Because God made the material and is immanent within (that is, indwells) the created order, creation itself has a spiritual dimension. Likewise man in his materiality is spiritual. And his task in the world as the image-bearer of God is a spiritual task, which, by virtue of Creation, cannot be separated from the material nature of his life in the world.

However, because man exercised freedom of choice and chose to unfold his life in a direction away from God, he has not fulfilled the original intention of God for His creation. A second Adam has therefore entered history. God Himself has become incarnate in the person of the God-man Jesus Christ. This event occurred within history and inaugurated a new beginning for man, creation, and history. It was God's way of destroying the dominion of death and the power of sin. Christ began a new order within the old. Those who are in Christ by faith become a part of His body, the church. The church is a visible and historical organism of people who by their lives and deeds give witness to the new creation. This is a historical task. It takes place in the midst of culture and history. And though it sometimes looks weak and feeble and may not appear to be "something new," it witnesses to the final goal of history, the new heavens and the new earth. The church therefore belongs to this *present creation* and this present history. It is a structure of life, the means through which God manifests Himself to the world.

A case for evangelical social responsibility must begin with Creation. Creation inaugurated history. History is the arena in which God's purposes are worked out. Man as the image-bearer of God is the agent through whom God works out His purposes. Man failed to do God's will. The Second Man has entered into history. His actions in history—life, death, resurrection—initiate a new beginning within history. Those who belong to this new beginning are called the church. They are now to fulfill God's purposes within history in every structure of life. And they look to the end of history, to the new heavens and the new earth.

Sin

The second general category into which a number of biblical-theological concerns fall is that of evil. In the first place, evil is not something inherent within the created order. Evangelicals avoid the heresy that the material is evil. God did not create evil. And since the creation results from an act of God's will, then the creation is good, as God Himself affirmed it to be. It follows that evil is not something material; evil is that which opposes God, that attempts to thwart His design and destroy His purposes in Creation. It can be seen as a violent force, an active energy that relentlessly seeks to pervert the will of God. God Himself is involved in a struggle with the powers of evil. And in this struggle real losses occur. Evil never creates, it never results in good, nor does it ever ultimately benefit those who are ruled by it. It is always a negation of the good, and therefore it always takes shape in radical opposition to God—for example, a revolt, a disobedience, or a resistance.

Evil is therefore known to us in history. It takes shape before our very eyes. It possesses and controls us. It shapes our lives and destroys our destiny. It perverts the image-character of our being. Because man chose evil rather than the will of God, he broke his ascent toward God and initiated a movement away from God, a desertion from the service of God's will. But sin was not just an option for the wrong direction; it was a change of affection and therefore a despiritualization of existence. Man began to love himself alone and thereby made himself the ultimate point of reference. Because personality is the "image of God," this image can be maintained only when man makes God his God and remains in constant communion with Him. Man shifted his point of reference and by the power of negation began the descent away from God.

The horror of this choice can be observed in its consequences in history. Because man is a being-in-history, his choice is reflected only too dramatically in his cultural unfolding. His dignity and task in the created order have not changed; only his allegiance has changed. But his allegiance is the source from which he acts. His commitment is now to himself, and the results of this are seen everywhere.

Sin and evil are not phantoms or mirages. They express themselves as actions—actions of individuals, groups, and nations. They permeate the structure of life. They control lives. They determine destinies.

All of man's wickedness is seen in his cultural unfolding. Sin becomes something more than personal—it expresses itself in the spirit of the age. And it is demonstrated in the multitudinous forms of alienation that occur between man and God, man and himself, man and man, and man and nature.

Because there is only one culture and one history, all mankind is affected by the presence of evil everywhere. There is no place to go where evil is not evident. No relationship, no institution, no facet of life is immune.

However, the kingdom of God is in our midst. This means that the rule of Christ is also everywhere present. Christ has already destroyed the power of sin and overcome death. Therefore those who are "in Christ" have the power to overcome sin. And this power is historical, for the "in Christ" crowd is gathered in the church. The church is no mere "spiritual" entity. It is spiritual, but it is also the people of God *in history*. These people are to have an influence on history, on cultural unfolding. The church proclaims the kingdom and is an instrument of the kingdom. As "salt" and "light," the church points beyond the present chaos and disharmony caused by sin to the ultimate restoration of all things in the new heavens and the new earth.

Redemption

The redemption brought by Jesus Christ is cosmic. It has to do with all of creation and with man. For this reason the soteriology of the early Fathers revolved around two axioms. The first axiom was that "only God can save," which emphasized the role of the Triune God in salvation. The Savior was no mere created being. He was God Himself—the incarnate Son. The second axiom was that "only that which is assumed is healed." This points to the teaching that God became fully man. He was not a mere shell in whom the divine Logos entered. Instead, Jesus Christ, though fully God and one with the Father, was fully man and one with humanity. He was no less human than Adam. Therefore salvation came not only by God but also by man. Only one who was completely God and completely man could save man. He is the cosmic Christ.

Since He is the cosmic Christ, He does not merely "save souls." His work affects the whole created order. The result of sin was death. As one man's disobedience brought all men under death (the entire cosmos is subject to disintegration), so one man's obedience brings life to all (even the creation waits for its release from bondage to decay—Romans 8:21).

Christ as the "second Adam" brought a new beginning to man and the whole creation. This is a biblical teaching that is often overlooked by Western individualists. The "new creation" is not merely individual but cosmic. Everything that is affected by sin is now affected by redemption. Healing is now possible between man and God, man and himself, man and other men, and man and nature. The disintegrating power of sin has been reversed by redemption.

Cosmic redemption is not only a salvation that lies beyound the present but also a salvation that begins in the present. That is, redemption, which took place in history, has a present historical side to it. The effect of redemption is to be manifested in history even as the effect of sin has been manifested in history. Those who are redeemed and belong to the body of Christ are to live their lives from a different viewpoint, grounded in God and His revelation and not in themselves and their selfish desires. For this reason their cultural unfolding will be different.

At this point the Holy Spirit takes on significance in the life of the believer and in the life of the church. The fruit of the Spirit is vastly different from the fruits of evil. The task and calling of redeemed man is to unfold culture in such a way that culture reflects the "new creation." Instead of violence, greed, injustice, and the like, the new man seeks to bring about peace, love, and justice. His vision of life and human culture and values is therefore radically different from the world's. His eye is fixed on the reality of the new heavens and the new earth, but his task is to make that reality present in the world.

Implications

This biblical theology (of which I have sketched only the framework) implies a number of things about social responsibility. In the first place, it is an inescapable fact that life in this world is *historical.* We belong to this world and cannot escape it. The unfolding of man's life is a cultural unfolding. That is, the consequences of living are evident in the events of history. In the second place, broadly speaking, there are only two basic allegiances that man can make. Either he moves away from God and therefore toward himself, or he moves toward God and away from selfish commitment. The decision to move toward or away from God has historical consequences and therefore cultural implications.

It is not as if one could see two distinct histories or cultures within cultural and world history. There is only one culture, one history. But there are two discernible "spirits" or "courses" or "rules" that control the hearts and minds of man and result in tensions that are experienced by man in the personal level and by men on a corporate level.

No one and no group (even the church) is purely evil or purely good. There is a residual element of evil in all Christians, and there is a considerable amount of good in all non-Christians. We are all caught in the cosmic tension between good and evil.

These realities point to the inescapable social, political, and cultural dimension of living. Man is a social being in history. He cannot be anything other than that. Consequently the church, which is both the corporate body of believers and a social entity within the world, cannot escape social responsibility. Even neglect or indifference must be seen as a way of dealing with social responsibility. It may not be the best way, but it is still a "way," because it has a direct bearing on history.

The question, then, is not "Do Christians have a social responsibility?" but "How may we best carry out our responsibility in culture?"

THREE CONSIDERATIONS

At this point we need to return to our historical models. Which of the models should Evangelicals adopt? Should all Evangelicals be separatists? Identifiers? Transformationalists? This is not an easy question to answer. I will set forth three considerations as a means of gaining a perspective on the question.

1. The basic thrust of each model is grounded in biblical teaching.
2. An emphasis on one of the models without adequate consideration of the others leads to an unbalanced approach.
3. The cultural situation sometimes demands or supports the emphasis of one model more than another.

The Basic Thrust

Our examination of the biblical roots of the three models bears out that each one is based on biblical teachings.

The separatists base their approach to culture on those Scriptures that stress the other-worldliness of the Christian life. They pattern themselves after Christ the suffering servant, the one whose power is in the weakness of the Cross. They look on themselves as a people who are strangers and pilgrims in an alien land. They take seriously the admonition that they are not to "love the world or the things of the world." Their concern is to fulfill the prescriptions of the Sermon on the Mount and to be those people whom Peter described as "a chosen race, a royal priesthood, a holy nation, God's own people." They fully expect to suffer, to be misunderstood, to be reviled, and to be persecuted for righteousness' sake. But none of this matters to them because this world is not their home.

The identifiers, on the other hand, stand on those Scriptures that portray the this-worldly character of the Christian life. They stress the Incarnation and the identification of God with the created order and with humanity represented by the Incarnation. They point to the fact that Jesus ate and drank with the "tax collectors and sinners." He was no recluse, no separatist. He was always "where the action was"—calling people to an affirmation of the abundant life. Even Paul insisted that "all things are lawful" and that Christians were to be obedient to the powers, upholding the state, praying for kings and emperors, and admonishing slaves and servants to be obedient to their masters.

The transformationalists also base their view on Scripture. For them, the gospel is the power not only to change individual lives but also to change the structures of life, to transform culture. Thus they stress the resurrected Christ, the one who reigns as Lord over the entire creation. They accent Paul's teaching that God was in Christ "to reconcile to himself all things, whether on earth or in heaven, making peace by the blood of his cross" (Col. 1:20). Their vision of the world is like that of the prophets who longed for the day when justice and peace would rule the land. They look for an expression of the new heavens and the new earth in the present world. And therefore they insist that the Christian's responsibility is to work for that day when God's will will be done "on earth as it is in heaven."

An Unbalanced Approach

Although each of the models is rooted in a basic biblical teaching, an overemphasis on any one can actually undermine and eventually distort the biblical idea.

For example, while the separatists correctly assert that we are not of this world, a misunderstanding of what is meant by that idea (resulting from an overemphasis on separation from the world) can lead to practices that are altogether heretical. The word *world* really means "course of this world" or "influence of evil." If the word is mistakenly taken to refer to the "structures of life," as it sometimes is, some wrong practices will result. An extreme result would be a view that the created order or the structures of creation are inherently evil. This results in an asceticism that denies the body and withdraws from the world. A more moderate attitude, but one that still denies the goodness of creation, sees all institutions (such as government) as instituted by God because of sin. The practical implication of such a view is that the Christian can have nothing to do with government because he belongs to "another order." The effect of this attitude is to deny that there is only one history and one culture and to divide man and his life into the secular and the sacred. The extreme separation that results from this view may give a Christian a sense of really belonging to another order, but it does so at the expense of recognizing his identification with this world and his calling to transform it through the gospel.

The identifiers may be tempted to go to the opposite extreme. In their eagerness to identify with the world, they may fail to appreciate the influence of evil within the structures of life and too quickly accept prevailing practices in culture, even patterning aspects of the Christian message after them. This error has happened often; the church becomes married to the culture, as it did in the Constantinian era, in Nazi Germany, and in American civil religion. The danger of this approach is that the church loses its prophetic stance. It loses its objectivity toward the culture and therefore often fails to function as the critic of culture, pointing to its evils and demanding repentance. It tends toward a soft and complacent Christianity that maintains the status quo.

An overemphasis on the transformational motif is often characterized by a Christian utopianism. The Christian message *is* characterized by hope, but to assume that the new creation can become a reality apart from the second coming of Christ fails to consider the radical nature of sin and the biblical view of history. Certainly the more liberal notion of transformation and the nineteenth-century hope that the twentieth would be the Christian century are mocked by the deplorable events of the twentieth century. A view of transformation that neglects the ever-present reality of man's sinful nature and assumes that man is getting better ignores the teaching on sin that lies behind the separational model. The recognition that man is sinful and that Christ's victory over evil will not be complete until He returns and puts evil under His feet forever moderates all utopian idealism.

The Cultural Situation

In spite of the dangers involved in emphasizing one model over the others, it may well be appropriate to do so within a given cultural situation.

For example, it certainly seems most appropriate that the church's emphasis during the pre-Constantinian period was on separation. After all, the culture was permeated by the worship of false gods. No matter where one turned—in education, in occupation, or in social intercourse—one was always confronted by the necessity of recognizing a pagan god if one was to function satisfactorily in that sphere. Obviously a Christian did not have many alternatives. The choice to serve God necessitated a clear repudiation of the Roman gods. And since their presence permeated almost all of life, the witness of separation had to be made in nearly every direction.

The same principle was somewhat true in the Constantinian age as well. Suddenly the church had the opportunity to purge society of paganism with the backing of the government that formerly had opposed it. What was the church to do? It identified with the structures of life and turned toward an involvement in official Roman life. In the pre-Constantinian days it was rare to find Christians in government-related occupations. But Christians in post-Constantinian Rome quickly entered government and all the vocations that were open to them.

As a result of this identification, a certain transformation began to occur in the Roman world. For example, the mission

techniques were not confrontational so much as transformational. Many pagan feast days and practices were Christianized and thereby transformed. The pagan day of the sun,
for instance, was transformed into the celebration of the
birth of Christ. Gradually society became Christianized.
When Rome fell, the monasteries carried this Christianized
view of Western culture into the medieval period and eventually gave us the golden era of the medieval synthesis under
Innocent III.

An awareness of these three considerations along with the
complexities they introduce to the problem of Christians in
culture, lead me to the following conclusion: *No one model
adequately describes the relationship of the Christian to society; on the
other hand, each of the models provides an insight into a facet of
Christian social responsibility.* Therefore I shall propose the
development of a new model that brings together the biblical
and historical truths of each of these three models into a single
and coherent whole. I call it the incarnational model.

AN INCARNATIONAL MODEL

The model of the Christian's relationship to the world is
found in Jesus Christ, God incarnate. In Jesus God entered
into human history and life and through His person and work
modeled the relationship that His body, the church, is to express to the world. He identified with the world; was separate
from the ideologies that rule it; and by His death, resurrection,
and second coming assured its transformation.

Christ Identified With the World

In the first place, Christ identified with the natural order.
He was, as the New Testament teaches and the creeds confess,
"fully man." He assumed our nature and became flesh and
blood. The early church's insistence that he was "born of a
virgin, suffered under Pontius Pilate, was dead and buried,
and on the third day rose again" was directed against all
Gnostic denials of the full humanity of Christ. The church has
always taught that He was one of us. He endured hunger,

loneliness, pain, temptation, and all other human emotions. The writer of Hebrews affirms that "we have not a high priest who is unable to sympathize with our weaknesses, but one who in every respect has been tempted as we are, yet without sinning" (4:15).

In the second place, Christ identified with the social order. He was a particular person in a particular culture. He was part of the Jewish culture of His time and freely moved within it. His customs of life were not different from the norm. His dress, mannerisms, and habits of life such as eating, drinking, traveling, and worshiping were all in keeping with the acceptable norms of the day (except when He wished to make a point against the Pharisees). He made friends with all classes of people: Nicodemus was wealthy; Levi was a hated tax collector; Luke was a physician; and Peter was a fisherman. He was involved in the religious life of the culture. He attended the synagogue, participated in the Passover, and prayed in the temple. He was involved in the social life of society, such as the wedding in Cana. Because of His involvement in life, the Pharisees accused Him of being "a glutton and a drunkard, a friend of tax collectors and sinners" (Matt. 11:19). Furthermore, it appears that He supported the government. When He was asked, "Is it lawful to pay taxes?" He answered, "Render therefore to Caesar the things that are Caesar's" (Matt. 22:17,21).

Christ's identification with the world is not something that is "above" the world, nor a mere "running alongside" the world. Rather, it is His presence in the world. It is the kingdom of God "in the midst of you" (Luke 17:21).

By implication, the Christian church (which is His body) must be present to the world in the way in which Christ identified Himself with society. We are the instruments of His kingdom and witnesses to it. For this reason we must not withdraw our presence from any legitimate structure of society. All dimensions of life—including the social, political, economic, educational, and entertaining—are to be affirmed by Christians. Society belongs to God by virtue of Creation and has been sanctified by the presence of Christ within it. Our willingness to identify with the world as image-bearers of God dare not be less than that which Christ, the true and complete imprint of God, exemplified.

The following description of the second-century Christians, taken from *The Epistle to Diognetus,* is an example of what Christian identification in the world may look like:

> For the Christians are distinguished from other men neither by country, nor language, nor the customs they observe. For they neither inhabit cities of their own, nor employ a peculiar form of speech, nor lead a life which is marked by any singularity.[10]

Christ Was Separate From the Ideologies That Rule the World

The notion of separation may have physical implications as it did for John the Baptist and the monastics. They went into the desert and from that stance assumed a prophetic role toward society. In the life of Jesus, however, separation is more clearly defined as spiritual separation from the powers and idealogies that rule the world. He did not identify with what Paul calls "the course of this world . . . the prince of the power of the air, the spirit that is now at work in the sons of disobedience" (Eph. 2:2).

A casual reading of the New Testament is enough to convince the reader that Christ was continually confronted with the "powers." These "powers" are not so much the strengths of men and organizations, but forces that transcend the earthly. They are the powers of evil.

Yoder makes several observations that are important to note. They may be paraphrased as follows:

1. All the powers in the world were created by God. These powers were originally good and may be seen as "the reign of order among creatures, order which in its original intention is a divine gift." They are the norms and structures in which life is to be lived.

2. These powers have rebelled against God and are now fallen. This fallenness is evident in their claiming to be idols. They "have succeeded in making men serve them as if they were of absolute value."

3. Because these powers are part of the created order *we cannot live without them.*[11]

In an attempt to be more concrete about these structures, Yoder defines them as "religious structures (especially the religious undergirdings of stable ancient and primitive societies), intellectual structures ('ologies and 'isms), moral structures (codes and customs), political structures (the tyrant, the market, the school, the courts, race and nation)."[12] We may add to this list all those structures of life in which we constantly engage. The point is that because of the Fall *all* of the structures of existence have been inverted by the evil one. Instead of being the natural servants of man, they became the powers that man serves.

An example of this may be found in the power of material possessions. The structure of economics is simply a reality of life. In order to live, man must have his basic needs for food, shelter, and clothing met. There is nothing wrong with meeting these needs. The structure of creation is made up in such a way that material goods are available. But because of the radical nature of fallenness, man and the structure of economics have been altered to the extent that money may become no longer the servant of man but his master. Man may become controlled by the power of money. He may exchange it for God and make its acquisition his goal in life. Money and material possessions become a thing of ultimate value. The whole course of a person's life may be in the service of money. Man becomes a slave to money.

Jesus confronted the power that money and material possessions hold over man. In the synoptic Gospels one out of ten verses deals with the problem of the rich and the poor. Jesus demanded that His followers make a radical break with the service of money. He insisted that "you cannot serve God and mammon" (Matt. 6:24) and His own life was an example of His teaching—He incarnated His own message.

Although a radical break with money is a major concern of Jesus, it is only *one* of a number of concerns. Money is one of five prominent issues that recur in the demand Christ makes on His followers. The others include a break with reputation, violence, family, and "religion."

At bottom, the issue against the powers is the problem of idolatry. Jesus was truly free because He served the Father, and although He lived in the midst of the structures and in constant relationship to the powers, He never lived in the service of the powers. By His life and teaching He witnessed against the powers and the hold they have on man when they become man's god.

In today's world Christians and the church live under the constant temptation to idolize the structures of life. We make them our saviors. We worship them by serving them. The devil's desire is to pervert our lives in such a way that our cultural unfolding reflects our commitment to selfishness, greed, injustice, and the like—all of which come from the power and influence of evil. Against this, the evangelical advocates *separation*. We are to separate ourselves not only from a commitment to evil but from the support of evil in all areas of life. Evil finds its way into all the structures of existence, even the church. Christians must take a prophetic stance toward the presence of evil in all its forms, both personal and corporate. The powers of materialism, sensualism, greed, war, hate, oppression, and injustice are not to rule the Christian; wherever they express themselves, they are to be fought.

Again, a good example of this life style is found in the description of the second-century Christians in *The Epistle to Diognetus:*

> They dwell in their own countries, but simply as sojourners. As citizens, they share in all things as if foreigners. Every foreign land is to them as their native country, and every land of their birth as land of strangers. They marry, as do all [others]; they beget children; but they do not destroy their offspring. They have a common table, but not a common bed. They are in the flesh but they do not live after the flesh. They pass their days on earth, but they are citizens of heaven. They obey the prescribed laws, and at the same time surpass the laws by their lives. They love all men, and are persecuted by all. They are unknown and condemned; they are put to death, and restored to life. They are

poor, yet make many rich; they are in lack of all things, and yet abound in all; they are dishonoured, and yet in their very dishonour are glorified. They are evil spoken of, and yet are justified; they are reviled, and bless; they are insulted, and repay the insult with honour; they do good, yet are punished as evil-doers. When punished, they rejoice as if quickened into life; they are assailed by the Jews as foreigners, and are persecuted by the Greeks; yet those who hate them are unable to assign any reason for their hatred.[13]

By the death, resurrection, and second coming of Christ the transformation of the world is assured

The incarnation of God in Christ was a prelude to death. Any discussion of the Incarnation that attempts to build a theology without recognition of the relationship of the Incarnation to the death, resurrection, and second coming of Christ is inadequate. It is all of a single piece and must be treated that way.

In the first place, it must be recognized that the death and resurrection of Christ destroys the sovereignty the powers hold over man. The apostle Paul specifically teaches this in reference to the power of death in 1 Corinthians 15. More specifically, Paul refers to the blow that Christ's death rendered to the powers in the complementary verbs in Colossians 2:15: "He disarmed the principalities and the powers and made a public example of them, triumphing over them in him." The explanation of these terms has been powerfully set forth by Berkhof in *Christ and the Powers:*

> By the cross (which must always, here as elsewhere, be seen as a unit with the resurrection) Christ abolished the slavery which, as a result of sin, lay over our existence as a menace and an accusation. On the cross He *"disarmed"* the Powers, "made a public example of them and thereby triumphed over them." Paul uses three different verbs to express more adequately what happened to the Powers at the cross.
>
> He "made a public example of them." It is precisely in the crucifixion that the true nature of the Powers has come to light. Previously they were accepted as the most basic and ultimate realities, as the gods of the world. Never had it been perceived, nor could it have been perceived, that this belief was founded on deception. Now that the true God appears on earth in Christ, it becomes apparent that the Powers are inimical to Him, acting not as His instruments but as His adversaries. The

scribes, representatives of the Jewish law, far from receiving
gratefully Him who came in the name of the God of the law,
crucified Him in the name of the temple. The Pharisees, per-
sonifying piety, crucified Him in the name of piety. Pilate, rep-
resenting Roman justice and law, shows what these are worth
when called upon to do justice to the Truth Himself. Obviously, "none of the rulers of this age," who let themselves be
worshipped as divinities, understood God's wisdom, "for had
they known, they would not have crucified the Lord of glory"
(I Cor. 2:8). Now they are unmasked as false gods by their
encounter with Very God; they are made a public spectacle.

Thus Christ has "triumphed over them." The unmasking
is actually already their defeat. Yet this is only visible to men
when they know that God Himself has appeared on earth in
Christ. Therefore we must think of the resurrection as well as of
the cross. The resurrection manifests what was already accomplished at the cross: that in Christ God has challenged the
Powers, has penetrated into their territory, and has displayed
that He is stronger than they.

The concrete evidence of this triumph is that at the cross
Christ has "disarmed" the Powers. The weapon from which
they heretofore derived their strength is struck out of their
hands. This weapon was the power of illusion, their ability to
convince men that they were the divine regents of the world,
ultimate certainty and ultimate direction, ultimate happiness
and ultimate duty for small, dependent humanity. Since Christ
we know that this is illusion. We are called to a higher destiny:
we have higher orders to follow and we stand under a greater
protector. No powers can separate us from God's love in Christ.
Unmasked, revealed in their true nature, they have lost their
mighty grip on men. The cross has disarmed them: wherever it
is preached, the unmasking and the disarming of the Powers
takes place.[14]

In the second place, Christian eschatology recognizes
that the *completion* of Christ's work against the powers will not
occur until the Second Coming. John provides a description of
the final judgment of Satan and the powers in the Book of
Revelation. After death and Hades are thrown into the lake of
fire, the new heavens and the new earth will become visible. In
this new Jerusalem, this restoration of paradise, all things will
be new. The devil will "deceive the nations no more" (20:3).

Because Christ has broken the power of sin over man,
man is free not to be a slave to the powers. The biblical
allusions to new life in Christ affirm this principle throughout
the New Testament. In Romans Paul reminds Christians that

"having been set free from sin," they have "become slaves of righteousness" (6:18). In Galatians he describes this new relationship as a "walk by the spirit" (5:16,25) as opposed to a walk that grows out of the "desires of the flesh" (v. 16). And the Christians in Colossae are reminded that they have "put off what is earthly" (3:5) and "put on the new nature" (v. 10).

Man has been set free so that he can choose not to serve the powers. But what about the creation? Is the creation still in bondage to the fallen state of the powers? Paul answers this question in Romans 8. The creation has not yet been set free. It "waits with eager longing . . . because the creation itself will be set free from its bondage to decay and obtain the glorious liberty of the children of God" (vv. 19-21). In the meantime both man and creation live in the hope of ultimate redemption, and it is in this hope that "we are saved" (v. 24).

Today Christians live in the recognition that the powers have been disarmed and that Christ will ultimately destroy all evil. Christ's power over evil is both a present reality and a future hope. Consequently we are called to a social involvement that seeks to transform the present culture, moving it toward a greater approximation of the ideal. We ought not to expect a utopia to result. But we ought to believe that change is possible and that working for this change is a way of witnessing to the ultimate reality of God's kingdom. The Christian hope that sin will be destroyed and peace will reign is more than a dream. It is a task that we are to work toward even though we know it will be universally realized only by the consummation of Christ's work in His second coming.

My conclusion is that the Incarnation is the center point from which to reflect on the role of the Christian in the world. As a revelation of the Father, Christ was *identified* with the natural and social order, He was *separate* from the powers of evil that rule the course of the world, and He began the *transformation* of the world in His death and resurrection—a transformation that will be completed in His second coming. *This three-sided view of reality points to the relationship that exists between the Christian and the world.*

How Are We to Live?

The Christian lives in this world *in a state of tension between the yes and the no.*

The statement above demands some clarification. We will understand this definition best if we keep in mind the contrast that the Book of Revelation draws between Babylon and Jerusalem. Babylon is the *no* (separation). Jerusalem is the *yes* (transformation). We live in a state of tension between the two (identification).

The point is that there is only *one* culture, and both Babylon and Jerusalem are present within it. Babylon represents all that we are called to reject. It carries the full weight of all the fallenness of humanity. It is represented not only in the wickedness of individuals but also in the corporate wickedness of the institutions and organizations of man. The Christian is called to be a *no* to Babylon! Jerusalem, on the other hand, is the eschatological hope in the midst of the world. It points beyond the present to the future. It is found in every human expression of love, justice, and righteousness and is expressed here and there within the institutions and organizations of man. The Christian and the church as a corporate body within the world are called to be a *yes* to Jerusalem. They are to be the presence of Jerusalem in the world now.[15]

Obviously there are different levels of being no. Even among those who identify themselves as separatists, there are strong differences of opinion. Should Christians live on a poverty level? Should Christians band themselves together in communities? Is it enough to live a frugal existence? To what extent should Christians speak out against the overabundant consumption of food, energy, and other resources? How does our personal and corporate rejection of evil take shape and to what extent? There is no universal consensus on the exact way or level on which Christians and the church are to be the no.

On the other hand, there are many different levels of being yes. Even among those who identify themselves as transformationalists, there are strong differences of opinion.

Should we infiltrate existing structures and function with power through love? Should we begin new human structures and organizations that are controlled by the church or by those who are working for the kingdom? What can we expect? Can we hope for a national transformation? Will transformation be permanent or temporary?

The life of the Christian in the world is very complex. Because we live in tension between the yes and the no we are involved in the very thing we seek to be against. Although we speak strongly against moral, social, and political abuses, we participate in them. We abhor war, yet pay taxes; we cry for the hungry, yet overeat. We speak out against lust, yet lust. Obviously there are different levels of consistency, but the tension is still there. Furthermore, because we live in tension between the yes and the no we fail to accomplish the very goals we claim to live by. We live by the goals of the kingdom, but we fail to incarnate them completely because we are still sinners. We claim love, but often act unlovingly; we claim selflessness, but often act with selfish motives; we claim to be just and honest, but often act without honesty and justice.

The fact that we live in tension, however, does not invalidate our calling to be the yes and the no. It simply recognizes our inability to completely fulfill the ideal. It recognizes that the ideal has been fulfilled in Christ and that our calling as the body of Christ is to represent Christ in the world. But because we live on this side of our individual and corporate perfection we live somewhere between a complete no and a complete yes.

In practice this means that *there is no single way to fulfill our cultural task.* Four considerations will help in understanding this statement.

First, no model is so complete in itself that it does not also contain the others. For example, many Evangelicals are choosing to make their witness today through the *separational* approach. They gather in communities, they make prophetic statements regarding national and international policies, and they point out social problems that exist around the world and call for action. But this is never done apart from an *identifica-*

tion with the very thing they are against. They may be against
white supremacy, but many of their communities are exclusively white; male domination, but many are male; hunger,
but many overeat; pollution, but most drive cars that pollute;
poverty, but they live, if they are Americans, in the richest
nation in the world. Nor can the separatists avoid the *transformationalist* motif, either. They are interested in improving the
world situation by alleviating poverty, changing laws to make
them more just, and the like. The point is that the three models are always present in every social approach to one degree
or another.

Second, because cultures are different and the situation in
history changes from time to time, it is necessary to have
different models. This may be seen, for example, in the cultural differences between the pre-Constantinian and the Constantinian cultures. The pre-Constantinian culture was
oriented around the service of the Roman gods. It was difficult
for a Christian to be involved in certain trades and other
aspects of culture without giving homage to the emperor as a
god or affirming the existence and power of one or more of the
many gods that ruled the life of the average citizen. In this
context, it was necessary for Christians to develop a strong
separational stance. Their belief in Jesus Christ put them at
odds with their culture. On the other hand, when Constantine
confessed the faith a drastic cultural shift began. Soon occupations and cultural activities that were once off limits were
purged of their demonic associations. They became areas in
which Christians could feel free to participate. Similar cultural
situations still exist today. Obviously the church in Communist countries will look more like the separatistic model
than any other. And the church in a Western country will look
more like an identificational or transformational model. No
one model is the correct model for all times and all places.

Third, the fact that the Christian lives in tension between
the yes and the no is never to be used as an excuse against
social involvement. In fact, a single-minded separatist or
transformationalist may be more apt to be active socially than

an identifier. (We may see this single-mindedness as a calling.) Those who tend to identify with culture are not true to biblical Christianity if their identification is without the yes and the no. No matter how open a culture may be toward the church, it is never neutral. There are elements of the demonic within every culture. Against these the Christian and the church must speak and be a decisive no. And there are within every culture means through which the transformation of culture effected through the work of Jesus Christ may be expressed. In these areas the Christian and the church must be a decisive yes. The tension between the yes and the no must never be reduced to a comfortable complacency with the status quo.

Fourth, the tension between the yes and the no may never be used to support compromise with evil elements in one's culture. Christians and the church are always susceptible to alignments that are not carefully thought through. The power of cultural change, for example, may lure the church into its grip and create a situation in which the church uncritically approves cultural attitudes. Compromise is certainly seen in the support the German church gave to Hitler, in the emergence of American civil religion, and in the current efforts by some churchmen to legitimatize homosexual practice and marriages within the church. By being sensitive to the Holy Spirit and biblical teaching, the church must remain ever alert to the corroding and debilitating influence that anti-Christian cultural standards may exert toward Christian values and commitments.

CONCLUSION

In the biblical section I have set forth the argument that Christianity is not only personal, but also social. In the historical section I have shown the various ways in which the church has attempted to fulfill her cultural mandate in history. In this chapter I have attempted to set forth some additional arguments in order to create a case for evangelical social responsibility. By way of summary, they are:

1. Historical. The evangelical impulse of the eighteenth and nineteenth centuries had a strong social emphasis. American evangelicalism traces its origins to this movement.
2. Theological. Evangelical theology that seeks to support historic Christianity must recognize that classical biblical theology supports Christian social involvement.
3. Incarnational. God in the flesh is the ultimate example of involvement with the world. When He came He fully identified with the structures of life by living among us; He was separate from the influence of evil and by His death and resurrection He vanquished evil and began a new creation.

If evangelical Christianity is to mature into a full expression of the Christian faith, it must pay more careful attention to the mandate concerning social involvement that God has given in Scripture, in the history of the church, and in the Incarnation.

Questions for Discussion

1. Scan this chapter and write down all those words and terms that are unfamiliar to you. Define them in your own words. What do these ideas have to do with the Christian in culture?
2. What evangelical groups are known for their social concern? What does your church do?
3. Summarize in your own words the theological basis for social action.
4. In this chapter I have argued for a social latitudinarianism. What are the advantages and disadvantages of this view? Is it biblical?
5. Read through the Gospels and find examples of Jesus' approach to social problems. Can you support the case for an incarnational model from the example of Jesus?

6. How can the life of Jesus be extended to the world through you? List specific ways in which you, through obedience to Christ, can incarnate Jesus' relationship to culture.
7. How can the life of Jesus be extended to the world through the church? List specific ways in which the church, through obedience to Christ, can incarnate Jesus in your immediate locality.

Further Reading

Cairns, Earle E. *Saints and Society*. Chicago: Moody, 1960.

Dayton, Donald. *Discovering an Evangelical Heritage*. New York: Harper, 1976.

Dennis, Lane T. *A Reason for Hope*. Old Tappan, N.J.: Revell, 1976.

Krass, Alfred. *Five Lanterns at Sundown: Evangelism in a Chastened Mood*. Grand Rapids: Eerdmans, 1978.

Kraybill, Donald B. *The Upside-Down Kingdom*. Scottdale: Herald, 1978.

Moberg, David. *The Great Reversal: Evangelism Versus Social Concern*. Philadelphia: Lippincott, 1972.

Mouw, J. Richard. *Political Evangelism*. Grand Rapids: Eerdmans, 1973.

_____. *Politics and the Biblical Drama*. Grand Rapids: Eerdmans, 1976.

Sider, Ronald. *Rich Christians in an Age of Hunger*. Downers Grove: InterVarsity Press, 1977.

Sider, Ronald, ed. *The Chicago Declaration*. Carol Stream: Creation House, 1974.

Stringfellow, William. *An Ethic for Christians and Other Aliens in a Strange Land*. Waco: Word, 1973.

Wallis, James. *Agenda for Biblical People*. Grand Rapids: Eerdmans, 1972.

Yoder, John Howard. *The Politics of Jesus*. Grand Rapids: Eerdmans, 1972.

Notes

Chapter 1

1. See Ron Sider, *The Chicago Declaration* (Carol Stream: Creation, 1974).
2. It is not my purpose to use this term in a technical theological sense. Rather, my interest is in capturing the vastness of Christ communicated through a number of biblical images and themes. The reader who is interested in reading more widely on the subject should see such works as Karl Barth, *Christ and Adam: Man and Humanity in Romans 5,* Translated by T. A. Smail (New York: Macmillan, 1968); George Buttrick, *Christ and History* (New York: Abingdon, 1963); Ivar Ashaim, ed., *Christ and Humanity* (Philadelphia: Fortress, 1970); Robert W. Smith, ed., *Christ and the Modern Mind* (Downers Grove: Inter-Varsity, 1972); Robert Hale, *Christ and the Universe;* Tielhard de Chardin and the Universe Series, edited by Michael Meilach (Chicago: Franciscan Herald, 1973); Oscar Cullmann, *Christ and Time: The Primitive Christian Conception of Time and History* (Philadelphia: Westminster, 1964); and Charles M. Laymon, *Christ in the New Testament* (New York: Abingdon, 1958).
3. For more detailed information on the term *culture,* see Thomas Stearns Eliot, *Notes Towards the Definition of Culture* (New York: Harcourt, Brace, 1949); John Joseph Honigmann, *Understanding Culture* (New York: Harper, 1963); Fredirick C. Gamst, ed., *Ideas of Culture: Sources and Uses* (New York: Holt, Rinehart and Winston, 1976); Alfred Louis Knoeber, *The Nature of Culture* (Chicago: University of Chicago Press, 1952); Leslie A. White, *The Concept of Culture* (Minneapolis: Burgess, 1973).
4. For more on the idea of models as a way of seeing different sides of truth, see Ian G. Barbour, *Myths, Models, and Paradigms: A Comparative Study in Science and Religion* (New York: Harper, 1974).

Chapter 2

1. For a more detailed definition of the relationship between Christianity and culture, see Emile Cailliet, *The Christian Ap-*

proach to Culture (Nashville: Abingdon-Cokesbury, 1953); Arthur Wallace Calhoun, *The Cultural Concept of Christianity* (Grand Rapids: Eerdmans, 1950); Henry Christopher Dawson, *The Historic Reality of Christian Culture* (New York: Harper, 1960); Thomas Stearns Eliot, *Christianity and Culture: The Idea of a Christian Society and Notes Towards the Definition of Culture* (New York: Harcourt, Brace, 1968).

2. I am obviously indebted to H. Richard Niebuhr, *Christ and Culture* (New York: Harper, 1956). Niebuhr lists five categories of Christ and culture—Christ against culture; Christ of culture; Christ above culture; Christ and culture in paradox; Christ the transformer of culture. While these are helpful categories, they are somewhat confusing because they do not allow for the vast differences that exist under each category. I have therefore delineated three general categories, each of which has a large variety of expression. For example, the identificational model includes approaches such as Constantinianism, Lutheranism, and civil religion. Although each of these expressions is quite different from the others, they may all be classified under the general identificational model because of their concurrence with culture.

Chapter 3

1. Very few commentators deal sufficiently with the cultural implications of these terms. Helpful comments are found in Calvin, *Genesis* (Grand Rapids: Eerdmans, 1948), pp. 91-100; and Robert Davidson, *Genesis 1–11* in the *Cambridge Bible Commentary* (Cambridge: University Press, 1973), pp. 23-26.

2. Abraham J. Heschel, *Between God and Man,* ed. Fritz A. Rothschild (New York: Harper, 1959), p. 234.

3. This is dealt with extensively in the discussion on Calvin. See chapter 7.

4. Rene Dubos, *So Human an Animal* (New York: Scribner, 1968).

5. There is an interesting and helpful exchange between Dubos and White in Ian G. Barbour, ed., *Western Man and Environmental Ethics* (Reading, Mass.: Addison-Wesley, 1973), chs. 2, 3, 5.

6. Davidson, *Genesis 1–11,* p. 40.

7. An interesting and helpful discussion of this theme is found in Frederick Elder, *Crisis in Eden: A Religious Study of Man and His Environment* (New York: Abingdon, 1970).

8. Gerhard Von Rad, *Old Testament Theology* (New York: Harper, 1962), 1:154.

9. Davidson, *Genesis 1–11,* p. 54.

10. Jacques Ellul, *The Meaning of the City* (Grand Rapids: Eerdmans, 1970), p. 4. An interesting interpretation of Cain is found on pp. 3-7.
11. Davidson, *Genesis 1–11*, p. 80.
12. See Elder, *Crisis in Eden*, for a helpful insight into the current nature of man's crisis.

Chapter 4

1. I follow the conclusions of George Eldon Ladd. See his books *The Presence of the Future* (1974), *The Gospel of the Kingdom* (1961), and *Crucial Questions About the Kingdom* (1952), all published by Eerdmans (Grand Rapids).
2. John Bright, *The Kingdom of God* (Nashville: Abingdon, 1953), p. 18.
3. Ibid., p. 28.
4. For a summary of the evidence of the kingdom as present in Jesus, see Norman Perrin, *The Kingdom of God in the Teaching of Jesus* (London: SCM, 1963), especially pp. 74ff.
5. For an argument on the present form of the kingdom, see Ladd, *Presence*, chs. 6, 7, and 8.
6. See Herman Ridderbos, *The Coming of the Kingdom* (Philadelphia: Presbyterian and Reformed, 1962), pp. 61-70.
7. See Ladd, *Presence*, ch. 13.
8. Ladd develops this idea at length; see *Presence*, pp. 59ff.
9. For a thorough discussion of the relation between the kingdom and the church, see Wolfhart Pannenberg, *Theology and the Kingdom* (Philadelphia: Westminster, 1966), ch. 2.
10. Ladd, *Presence*, ch. 11.
11. Ibid., p. 262.
12. Ladd, *Gospel*, p. 115.
13. For an expansion of this problem see Ladd, *Presence*, ch. 12, and Pannenberg, *Theology*, ch. 3.
14. Ladd, *Presence*, p. 291.

Chapter 5

1. For an elaboration of this theme see William Stringfellow, *An Ethic for Christians and Other Aliens in a Strange World* (Waco: Word, 1973).
2. The fact that not all early Christians are to be regarded as separational has been set forth by Robert M. Grant in *Early Christianity and Society* (New York: Harper, 1977).
3. For an elaboration of church-and-state relations see Robert M. Grant, *The Sword and the Cross* (New York: Macmillan, 1955).

4. *Against Heresies*, iv. 36. Unless otherwise indicated, all refer-
    ences to the early church fathers are taken from *The Ante-Nicene
    Fathers* (Grand Rapids: Eerdmans, 1971), hereafter cited as
    Fathers.
5. *The First Apology, Fathers*, ch. 17.
6. Ibid.
7. iii, *Fathers*, ch. 15.
8. *Apology, Fathers*, ch. 15.
9. v, *Fathers*, ch. 24.
10. Cyril C. Richardson, ed., *Early Christian Fathers*, The Library of
    Christian Classics, vol. 1 (Philadelphia: Westminster, 1953).
11. *Didache, Fathers*, ch. 1.
12. See Acts 8:27; 10:1; 13:12; 16:27-34; 18:8; Phil. 4:22; Rom.
    16:10-11.
13. Burton Scott Easton, ed., *The Apostolic Tradition* (Hamden,
    Conn.: Archon Books, 1962), ch. 16.
14. Ibid.
15. *On Idolatry, Fathers*, ch. 19.
16. *On Shows, Fathers*, ch. 8.
17. *A Plea, Fathers*, ch. 35.
18. *The Passing of Peregrinus, Fathers*, ch. 13.
19. *Apology, Fathers*, ch. 14.
20. Philadelphia: Fortress, 1974, p. 1.
21. *Apology, Fathers*, ch. 15.
22. Ibid.
23. Richardson, *Early Christian Fathers, An Epistle to Diognetus*,
    ch. 5.
24. Ibid., ch. 6.
25. Ibid.
26. Franklin Littell, *The Anabaptist View of the Church* (Boston: Starr
    King Press, 1958), p. xvii.
27. For the various types of Anabaptists and for a good review of
    their history, see George H. Williams. *The Radical Reformation*
    (Philadelphia: Westminster, 1962), and William R. Estep, *The
    Anabaptist Story* (Grand Rapids: Eerdmans, 1975).
28. Littell, *Anabaptist View of the Church*, pp. 47ff.
29. Ibid., pp. 64-72.
30. For further elaboration of this idea, see Robert Friedmann, *The
    Theology of Anabaptism* (Scottdale, Pa.: Herald, 1973), pp.
    36-48.
31. For the complete text of this confession (trans. John C.
    Wenger), see *The Mennonite Quarterly Review*, 19 (October,
    1945): 247-53.
32. See Friedmann, *Theology*, pp. 39-40.

33. Section IV, point 70, as quoted in Friedmann, *Theology,* pp. 39-40.
34. Robert Friedmann, "On Mennonite Historiography and on Individualism and Brotherhood," *The Mennonite Quarterly Review,* 18 (April, 1944): 121.
35. Robert R. Kreider, "Anabaptists and the State," in Guy F. Hershberger, ed., *The Recovery of the Anabaptist Vision* (Scottdale, Pa.: Herald, 1957), p. 189.
36. Article 6.
37. Kreider, "Anabaptists and the State," p. 187.
38. Article 6.
39. See J. Lawrence Burkholder, "The Anabaptist Vision of Discipleship," in Hershberger, *Recovery,* pp. 135-51.
40. Peter Klassen, *The Economics of Anabaptism 1525-1560* (London: Nouton, 1964), p. 43.
41. Harold S. Bender, "The Anabaptist Vision," in Hershberger, *Recovery,* p. 51. See also James M. Stayer, *Anabaptists and the Sword* (Lawrence, Kan.: Coronado, 1972).
42. Harold S. Bender, "The Pacifism of the Sixteenth Century Anabaptists" *Church History XXIV* (1955), pp. 119-31.
43. Harold S. Bender, *The Anabaptists and Religious Liberty in the 16th Century* (Philadelphia: Fortress, 1970, pp. 2-3.
44. For a discussion of different kinds of Christian communities see Donald G. Bloesch, *Wellsprings of Renewal* (Grand Rapids: Eerdmans, 1974), and David and Neta Jackson, *Living Together in a World Falling Apart* (Carol Stream, Ill.: Creation House, 1974).
45. Grand Rapids: Eerdmans, 1970, p. 94.
46. Ibid., p. 108.
47. Notre Dame: Ave Maria, 1973, see pp. 18-26.
48. Michael Harper, *A New Way of Living* (Plainfield, N.J.: Logos, 1973), p. 8.
49. *The Joyful Community* (Baltimore: Penguin, 1971), p. 33.
50. Harper, *New Way,* p. 86.
51. *New Covenant* magazine, December 1971, p. 13.
52. Vernard Eller, *The Simple Life* (Grand Rapids: Eerdmans, 1973), p. 43.
53. An unpublished thesis, George Williams College, Downers Grove, Illinois.
54. Ibid., p. 38.

Chapter 6

1. *Christianity and Classical Culture* (New York: Oxford University, 1957), pp. 177-78.

2. See the most pertinent section of this decree in Henry Bettenson, *Documents of the Christian Church* (London: Oxford, 1963),
2nd ed., pp. 22-23.

3. Ibid.

4. Ibid.

5. For an expansion of these points, see Andrew Alfoldi, *The Conversion of Constantine and Pagan Rome*, trans. Harold Mattingly
(Oxford: Clarendon, 1948).

6. *Oration*, x.

7. v. 5.

8. v. 7.

9. *Christianity and Classical Culture*, p. 196.

10. Bettenson, *Documents*, p. 31.

11. Gerhard Ebeling, *Luther: An Introduction to His Thoughts*, trans.
R. A. Wilson (Philadelphia: Fortress, 1970), p. 25.

12. Martin Luther, "Temporal Authority: To What Extent It
Should Be Obeyed" (1523), in *Luther's Works*, 45 (Philadelphia: Fortress, 1971), pp. 85-87. My analysis of Luther's two-
kingdom theory is based on this document.

13. There is a difference between Luther's early views and his later
views. I am setting forth only his later, more mature thought
on the question. An excellent work, documenting Luther's
developing thought, is F. Edward Cranz, *An Essay on the Development of Luther's Thought on Justice, Law, and Society* (Cambridge:
Harvard University, 1959).

14. For an excellent study of Luther's two kingdoms, see Paul
Althaus, *The Ethics of Martin Luther* (Philadelphia: Fortress,
1972), ch. 4.

15. "Temporal Authority," p. 88.

16. For Luther's understanding of creation and natural law, see
Althaus, *Ethics*, ch. 2.

17. For a brief but helpful analysis of the Christian's struggle with
himself, see Althaus, *Ethics*, ch. 1.

18. "Temporal Authority," p. 91.

19. For a helpful insight into Luther's understanding of the spiritual and civil use of the law, see his comments on Galatians 3,
Luther's Works, 26:335-51.

20. "Temporal Authority," p. 89.

21. Ibid., p. 92.

22. Ibid., p. 94.

23. *Luther's Works*, 21:3-294.

24. For a discussion of Luther's teaching on this point, see Ebeling,
Luther, ch. 12.

25. See "A Sermon on the Estate of Marriage" (1519), in *Luther's*

Works, 44:7-14, and "On Marriage Matters" (1530), in *Luther's Works*, 46: 265-320.

26. Luther felt that the church's responsibility is to proclaim God's will for marriage. Marriage is an ordained institution of Creation, and not a matter of the church.

27. See Luther's interpretation of Psalm 127 and Psalm 128 in *D. Martin Luther's Werke*, Briefwechsel (Weimar, 1930-1948), pp. 202ff., pp. 278ff.

28. *Luther's Works*, 21:12ff.

29. In addition to "Temporal Authority," see Luther's "Commentary on Psalm 82" (1530), *Luther's Works*, 13:41-72; his "Commentary on Psalm 101," *Luther's Works*, 13:145-224; and his "Commentary on the Song of Solomon," Weimar 31, pp. 586-769.

30. The Christian is also obliged to support the state in any war it may wage for the purpose of defending its subjects against injustice and violence. Waging war against aggressors and others who threaten the peace of the state is a work of love because it ensures justice and preserves the peace. Implicit in Luther's understanding is the assertion that any aggressive war by a state is wrong and should not be supported by Christians. An aggressive war is waged not for the purpose of keeping peace and order but for selfish gain, to the destruction of peace and order.

31. For a discussion of Luther's view of the church see Werner Elert, *The Structure of Lutheranism*, trans. Walter A. Hansen (St. Louis: Concordia, 1962), chap. 20.

32. New York: Harper, 1974, pp. 14-18.

33. Jean-Jacques Rousseau, *The Social Contract and Discourses*, trans. and ed. G. D. H. Cole (New York: Dutton, 1950), p. 139.

34. For a detailed examination of this transition, see Ernst H. Kantorowicz, "*Pro Patria Mori* in Medieval Political Thought," *The American Historical Review*, 56 (April 1951): 472-92.

35. "A Model of Christian Charity," in H. S. Smith, R. T. Handy, and Lefferts A. Loetscher, *American Christianity: An Historical Interpretation with Representative Documents* (2 vols., New York: Scribner, 1960-63), 1:102.

36. For an excellent brief survey of this development, see Robert T. Handy, "The American Messianic Consciousness: The Concept of the Chosen People and Manifest Destiny," *Review and Expositor*, Winter 1976, pp. 47-58.

37. New York: Lippincott, 1970.

38. Ibid., pp. 32-33.

39. For an expansion on these ideas, see Martin E. Marty, *The New Shape of American Religion* (New York: Harper, 1959) and *The Pro & Con Book of Religious America* (Waco: Word, 1975).

Chapter 7

1. See also Isaiah 43:1ff.; 42:5-6; 54:5; Psalm 74, 89, 93, 95, 135, 136; Amos 4:12ff.; Jeremiah 33:25ff.; 10:16; 27:5; 32:17; Malachi 2:10. All these passages bring creation and redemption together. What is redeemed is not just "souls," but the whole created order.
2. Augustine, *The City of God*, ed. David Knowles (Baltimore: Penguin, 1972), xiv. 28. 593.
3. Ibid., xv. 2. 596.
4. John Neville Figgis, *The Political Aspects of St. Augustine's 'City of God'* (Gloucester: Peter Smith, 1963), p. 51.
5. Augustine, *City of God*, iv. 3. 138.
6. Ibid., iv. 4. 139.
7. Ibid., xx. 9. 915.
8. Ibid., xx. 9. 914.
9. Ibid., ii. 9. 916.
10. Figgis, *Augustine's 'City of God,'* pp. 79-80.
11. See H. Richard Niebuhr, *Christ and Culture* (New York: Harper, 1956), pp. 215-16.
12. See Brian Tierney, *The Crisis of Church and State 1050-1300* (Englewood Cliffs: Prentice-Hall, 1964), p. 13.
13. John Calvin, *Institutes of the Christian Religion*, i. 16. 1.
14. Henry Van Til, *The Calvinistic Concept of Culture* (Philadelphia: Presbyterian and Reformed, 1959), p. 53.
15. Ibid., p. 161.
16. André Biéler, *The Social Humanism of Calvin* (Richmond: John Knox, 1964), p. 18.
17. Ibid., p. 20.
18. Ibid.
19. William Mueller, *Church and State in Luther and Calvin* (Nashville: Broadman, 1954), p. 127.
20. *Institutes*, iv. 20. 2.
21. Ibid., 4.
22. Ibid., 9.
23. Biéler, *Social Humanism*, p. 23.
24. W. Fred Graham, *The Constructive Revolutionary* (Richmond: John Knox, 1971), pp. 61-63.
25. Biéler, *Social Humanism*, p. 31.
26. Graham, *Constructive Revolutionary*, p. 75.
27. Biéler, *Social Humanism*, p. 43.

28. Ibid., p. 45.
29. Graham, *Constructive Revolutionary*, p. 83.
30. Biéler, *Social Humanism*, p. 51.
31. Ibid., p. 51.
32. Monika Hellwig, "Liberation Theology: An Emerging School," *Scottish Journal of Theology* 30:138.
33. Gustavo Gutierrez, *A Theology of Liberation* (Maryknoll, N.Y.: Orbis, 1973), p. x.
34. Ibid., p. 151.
35. See also Rene Lawrentin, *Liberation, Development and Salvation*, trans. Charles Underhill Quinn (Maryknoll, N.H.: Orbis, 1972), especially pp. 63-84.
36. Gutierrez, *Theology of Liberation*, p. 193.
37. Ibid., pp. 159-60.
38. For a discussion of the relation between history and liberation see, Jose Miguez Bonino, *Doing Theology in a Revolutionary Situation* (Philadelphia: Fortress, 1975), pp. 132-52.
39. Gutierrez, *Theology of Liberation*, p. 193.
40. For the development of liberation ethics see Denis Goulet, *A New Moral Order* (Maryknoll, N.Y.: Orbis, 1974).
41. Gutierrez, *Theology of Liberation*, p. 202.
42. Ibid., p. 172.
43. For an expansion of liberation and political theology see Dorothee Soelle, *Political Theology* (Philadelphia: Fortress, 1974), and J. G. Davies, *Christian Politics and Violent Revolution* (Maryknoll, N.Y.: Orbis, 1976).
44. Gutierrez, *Theology of Liberation*, p. 265.
45. Ibid., p. 267.
46. Ibid., p. 269.

Chapter 8

1. Earle E. Cairns, *Saints and Society* (Chicago: Moody, 1960), p. 30.
2. Ibid.
3. Donald Dayton, *Discovering an Evangelical Heritage* (New York: Harper, 1976), p. 4.
4. Ibid.
5. Quoted in Dayton, *Evangelical Heritage*, p. 18.
6. Ibid., p. 19.
7. Ibid., p. 28.
8. See David O Moberg, *The Great Reversal: Evangelism Versus Social Concern* (Philadelphia: Lippincott, 1972).
9. See Ronald Sider, *The Chicago Declaration* (Carol Stream: Creation House, 1974).

10. *The Ante-Nicene Fathers* (Grand Rapids: Eerdmans, 1971), i. 5. 26., hereafter cited as *Fathers*.
11. John Howard Yoder, *The Politics of Jesus* (Grand Rapids: Eerdmans, 1972), pp. 143-44.
12. Ibid., p. 145.
13. *Fathers*, i. 5. 21.
14. Quoted in Yoder, *Politics of Jesus*, pp. 149-50.
15. See William Stringfellow, *An Ethic for Christians and Other Aliens in a Strange Land* (Waco: Word, 1973).

General Index

Anabaptists: 86-89; on the church, 88, 91; definition of, 86-87; desire to restore primitive church, 87-88; eschatology of, 89, 95; on involvement in government, 94; radical discipleship of, 93, 94; religious liberty and, 96; on the state, 93; the two kingdoms, 89-93; on war, 88, 94, 95
Aristides, 81, 84-85
Augustine, 42
Augustine and *The City of God*: 138-144; on the church, 141, 142; Donatist controversy, 142-143; eschatology of, 142; on involvement in government, 140; on justice and the state, 140; the state, 139-140; the two cities, definition, 138-139

Bandung Conference, 154
Beecher, Lyman, 131
Bender, Harold S., 95-96
Berkhof, Hendrik, 193
Bieler, Andre, 147, 150, 152, 153
Blanchard, Jonathan, 173
Bright, John, 54, 55

Cairns, Earle E., 170, 172
Calvin, John: 36, 93, 144-153; on callings, 145-146; on the Christian and work, 152-153; the church, 147; concern for the poor, 147-148, 149, 150; on involvement in government, 149; man, sin, and salvation, 146-147; on money and property, 150-152; relation between church and state, 149; the state, 148-149; sovereignty of God, 145-146; on unification of religion and culture, 145

Chalcedon, Council of, 16, 113
Charlemagne, 143-144
Chicago Declaration, 13, 23-24, 175-176
Christian Community Movement: 96-102; church as community, 98-99; eschatology of, 98, 100; on private property, 99-101; radical discipleship in, 97-98; simplicity in personal and community life, 101-102; witness of, 99
Civil religion: 127-133; American civil religion, 130-133; business and, 132; definition of, 127-129; history of, 129-130; political conservatism and, 132-133
Cochrane, Charles Norris, 108, 111
Collistus, 85
Constantine I (the Great), 88, 108-110, 181
Constantinian church: 107-113; attitude toward state, 110-111; establishment of, 108; eschatology of, 110, 112; favored by state, 108-110; involvement in government, 112
Cyprian of Carthage, 141

Davidson, Robert, 39, 42, 46
Dayton, Donald, 172-173, 174
Delespesse, Max, 98
Didache, 82
Diognetus. See *Letter to Diognetus*
Dubos, Rene, 38

Ebeling, Gerhard, 113
Edict of Milan, 108
Edwards, Jonathan, 131
Eller, Vernard, 101

213

Scripture Index